THE UNNATURAL AND ACCIDENTAL WOMEN

Marie Clements

Talonbooks

Vancouver

Talonbooks
278 East First Avenue, Vancouver, British Columbia V5T 1A6
www.talonbooks.com

Sixth printing: September 2015

Typeset in New Baskerville
Printed and bound in Canada
on Forest Stewardship Council®-certified paper

Talonbooks gratefully acknowledges the financial support of the Canada Council for the Arts, the Government of Canada through the Canada Book Fund, and the Province of British Columbia through the British Columbia Arts Council and the Book Publishing Tax Credit.

Rights to produce *The Unnatural and Accidental Women*, in whole or in part, in any medium by any group, amateur or professional, are retained by the author. Interested persons are kindly requested to contact Marie Clements, P.O. Box 2662, Vancouver Main, Vancouver, British Columbia, V6B 3W8; tel: (778) 881-3801.

The Unnatural and Accidental Women was first published in *Staging Coyote's Dream: An Anthology of First Nations Drama in English* by Playwrights Canada Press in 2002.

Library and Archives Canada Cataloguing in Publication

Clements, Marie, 1962–
      The unnatural and accidental women / Marie Clements.

A play.
ISBN 0-88922-521-4

     I. Title.

PS8555.L435U55 2005   C812'.6   C2004-906435-5

ISBN-13: 978-0-88922-521-3

The Unnatural and Accidental Women was first presented on November 2, 2000 at the Firehall Arts Centre in Vancouver, B.C. with the following cast:

VALERIE .... Columpa Bobb
MAVIS .... Gloria May Eshkibok
THE BARBER .... Peter Hall
AUNT SHADIE .... Muriel Miguel
REBECCA .... Michelle St. John
RON .... Bill Croft
VIOLET .... Tasha Faye Evans
VERNA .... Sophie Merasty
THE WOMAN .... Michelle Olson
ROSE .... Christine Willes
THE BARBERSHOP WOMEN .... Dolores Dallas,
                              Adele Kruger &
                              Odessa Shuquaya

Co-Directors .... Donna Spencer &
                             Marie Clements
Set & Lighting Designer .... Robert Gardiner
                      (assisted by Kyla Gardiner)
Slide/Visual Designer .... Michelle Nahanee
Music Composition .... Ulali
Music Arrangement .... Simon Kendall
Costume Designer .... John Powell
                        (assisted by Lynn Hill)
Sound Designer .... Noah Drew
Assistant to the Directors .... Fif Fernandes
Stage Manager .... Deborah Ratelle
Technical Director .... James Proudfoot
Visual Technical Direction ...... Craig Alfredson

The Unnatural and Accidental Women is a play based on a true murder case in Vancouver that involved the deaths of at least ten women and many more "mystery" deaths of women in the East Hastings Street area unofficially referred to as "Skid Row." All the women were found dead with a blood-alcohol reading far beyond safe human consumption, and all the women were last seen with Gilbert Paul Jordan, a local barber who frequented the bars preying on primarily middle-aged Native women. The coroner's reports listed the cause of death for many of the women as "unnatural and accidental."

CHARACTERS:

REBECCA (ages 4 and 30): *Mixed blood/Native—a writer searching for the end of a story.*

ROSE (age 52): *English immigrant—a switchboard operator with a soft heart, but thorny.*

AUNT SHADIE (age 52): *Native—mother qualities of strength, humour, love, patience.*

MAVIS (age 42): *Native—a little slow from the butt down, but stubborn in life and memory.*

THE WOMAN (age 27): *Native—looks and moves like a deer.*

VALERIE (age 33): *Native—a big, beautiful woman proud of her parts.*

VERNA (age 38):	*Native—sarcastic but searching to do the right thing, the right way.*
VIOLET (ages 5 and 27):	*Native—an old spirit who grows younger to see herself again.*
THE BARBERSHOP WOMEN:	*A beautiful, sexy threesome that can move and sing.*
	MARILYN (age 25): Native
	PENNY (age 30): Native
	PATSY (age 40): Native
THE BARBER (ages 30s and 60s):	*White—short, balding, nice and creepy. Also transforms into THE MAN, THE ROMANTIC PARTNER, THE PILLOW, THE DRESSER, THE MAN'S SHADOW, THE AIRINE STEWARD, and 2ND FATHERLY MALE VOICE.*
RON (age 35):	*A cop—handsome, with a nice body and a good sense of humour. Also plays THE LOGGER, and is IT until he is RON.*

SFX VOICES:

EVAN (age 8):	*VALERIE's oldest son, wise and angry.*
TOMMY (age 5):	*VALERIE's youngest son, naive and sweet.*
THE OPERATOR:	*A polite but repetitive telephone recording.*
FATHERLY MALE VOICE:	*THE WOMAN's adopted father.*
"Can I buy you a drink?":	*THE BARBER's voice.*

ACT 1

Scenes involving the women should have a black-and-white picture feel that is animated by the bleeding-in of colour as the scene and their imaginations unfold. Colours of personality and spirit, life and isolation, paint their reality and activate their own particular landscape within their own particular hotel room and world. Their deaths are a drowning-down of hopes, despairs, wishes. The killer is a manipulative embodiment of their human need. Levels, rooms, views, perspectives, shadow, light, voices, memories, desires. RECECCA's journey through Act 1 should be a growing up through memory. Being in a memory, but present in time. Walking. Seeing. Time going by. Life—colour of memory and the searching. AUNT SHADIE and ROSE are on the top level from the beginning. In their own spaces and places. They are in their own world. Happy hunting ground and/or heaven.

Elements: Trees falling, falling of women, earth, water flowing/transforming.

ACT 2

Scenes in REBECCA's apartment are present and in Kitsilano, but reflect the symptoms of urban isolation even without being on Hastings Street.

Flow: Scenes of hearing, shadow-seeing, consciousness, unconsciousness of what is around us/within us.

DEATH BY ALCOHOL
The Vancouver Sun, October 22, 1988

"'She was found lying nude on her bed and had recent bruises on her scalp, noses, lips, and chin … There was no evidence of violence, or suspicion of foul play,' noted Coroner Glen McDonald."

" ——, a native Indian, had been drinking continuously for four days before she died … Coroner Larry Campbell concluded her death was 'unnatural and accidental.'"

" —— drank enough to kill her twice. That's the conclusion of a coroner's inquiry into the native Indian woman's death. She was found dead, lying face down on a foam mattress with a blanket covering her, in Jordan's barbershop … At the time of her death, Coroner Campbell said there was no indication of foul play."

"To get the blood-alcohol reading that —— had at the time of her death, experts say she would have had to drink about 40 ounces of hard liquor all at once. The mother of four died at Jordan's barbershop … Coroner Mary Lou Glazier concluded ——'s death was 'unnatural and accidental.'"

"'She had the highest blood-alcohol level reading of all the women.' … He believes Jordan was finally stopped because he killed his daughter, who was not an alcoholic and who has family that insisted police look into her death. 'He picked the wrong person. She was someone that someone cares about.' … No coroner's report has been issued."

ACT 1

SFX: A collage of trees whispering in the wind.

SLIDE: THE UNNATURAL AND ACCIDENTAL WOMEN

*SFX: The sound of a tree opening up to a split. A loud
crack—a haunting gasp for air that is suspended. The
sustained sound of suspension as the tree teeters.*

SLIDE: FALLING BACK—Beacon Hotel

*Lights dim up on a small room covered with the shadows of
tree leaves and limbs. Lights up on a LOGGER looking up at
a tree, handsaw in hand. He shouts across time.*

LOGGER:
TIM-BER ...

AUNT SHADIE:
Re-becca ...

*A big woman suddenly emerges from a bed of dark leaves.
Gasping, she bolts upright, unfallen. Nude, she rises,
leaving the image of herself in the bed. She follows the
sounds and images of the trees.*

**SLIDE: Rita Louise James, 52, died November 10,
1978 with a 0.12 blood-alcohol reading. No
coroner's report issued.**

9

SFX: Real sound of REBECCA slamming a glass of beer on her table.

SFX: The sound of trees moving in the wind increases.

SLIDE: TIMBER

Lights fade up on REBECCA as she sits, and thinks, and drinks at a round table with a red terry-cloth cover. She takes her pen and writes in her journal.

The LOGGER continues sawing ...

SFX: Sound of a long saw sawing under softly in lengths.

AUNT SHADIE walks through the forest, covered by the leaves / branches in them.

REBECCA:

Everything here has been falling—a hundred years of trees have fallen from the sky's grace. They laid on their backs trying to catch their breath as the loggers connected them to anything that could move, and moved them, creating a long muddy path where the ends of trees scraped the ground, whispering their last connection to the earth. This whispering left a skid. A skid mark. A row. Skid Row.

The LOGGER lays down his saw and picks up a chainsaw...

SFX: Sound of a chainsaw under.

Throughout—a blizzard of sawdust chips swarms the backdrop, covering AUNT SHADIE and tree parts. One by one, the trees have been carved into a row of hotels.

REBECCA:

Hotels sprung up instead of trees—to make room for the loggers. First, young men sweating and working under the sky's grace. They worked. They sweated. They fed their family for the Grace of God. And then the men began to fall. First, just pieces.

AUNT SHADIE:

Fingers ...

REBECCA:

... chopped down to the palm.

AUNT SHADIE:

Legs ...

REBECCA:

... chopped up to the thighs.

AUNT SHADIE:

Years ...

REBECCA:

... went by. You never knew what might be fallen. A tree. A man. Or, a tree on its way down deciding to lay on its faller like a thick and humorous lover, saying ...

AUNT SHADIE:

"Honey, I love you—we are both in this together. This is love till death do us part—just try and crawl out from under me."

REBECCA:

Some of the men survived their amorous lover. Rows of men sweet-talked that last fallen tree into moving an inch to get that human limb out. Maybe just a leg—or part of it. Whispering ...

AUNT SHADIE:

"God, if you just do this for me. Jesus, just get this log off me ... and ... "

REBECCA:
Well, a whole crew of men sitting in their rooms
drinking and thinking of the weight of that last tall love.

*The LOGGER finishes and looks around and looks right at
REBECCA. REBECCA mouths "I love you" to him silently.*

The LOGGER cups his ear and shouts towards her.

LOGGER:
Eh? (*he waves his hand a "never mind" and continues*)

REBECCA:
Saying "Eh"?

*The LOGGER continues the buzz with the chainsaw. Wood
chips blizzard on the backdrop. The chainsaw buzzes under
transforming to a bar buzz.*

AUNT SHADIE:
(*laughs*) Saying "Eh?" a lot. Could you repeat that? Their
voices yelling over the sound of the power saw buzzing
thirty years ago, or was it last year? Never mind, the buzz
rings in their ears just as the sawdust used to rest in their
belly buttons after a hard day's work. Honest work. A
tree for …

REBECCA:
… a thumb.

AUNT SHADIE:
A tree for a …

REBECCA:
… leg.

AUNT SHADIE:
A tree for their …

REBECCA:
… hearing.

AUNT SHADIE:

An honest trade made between a logger and his trees.
No malice between the two—just an honest respect for
the give and take of nature.

SFX: The full buzz of a bar under.

*The woodchip blizzard clears, and crudely made stumps that
look like bar stools remain behind her and deepen the look of
the bar—the Empress Hotel. AUNT SHADIE walks across the
bar but is also covered by it, in it.*

REBECCA:

Now the loggers sit like their lovers, the trees—they sit
like stumps, and drink, and think. And think the world
has gone to shit. They think of a time when cutting
down a tree was an honest job, a time when they all had
their good-looking limbs, a time when they were
respected by the tallest order, a time when drinking was
not an addiction.

*AUNT SHADIE turns up a flight of stairs as we watch her
shadow ascend.*

AUNT SHADIE:

And the women. Oh the women strolled by and took in
their young sun-baked muscles and happy cash.

REBECCA turns back to her journal.

REBECCA:

If you sit long enough, maybe everything becomes clear.
Maybe you can make sense of all the losses and find one
thing you can hold on to. I'm sitting here thinking of
everything that has passed, everyone that is gone, and
hoping I can find her, my mother. Not because she is my
first choice, but because she is my last choice and ... my
world has gone to shit.

She looks around the room and raises her glass.

Cheers ...

*Lights up on the same hotel room, as AUNT SHADIE takes
two old suitcases out from under her bed. She lies them on
the bed and opens them slowly, hesitantly. Cree words spill
out everywhere. She opens and closes the sound and begins
to laugh. Affectionately, she snaps them shut, picks them up
and walks towards the door and up. The suitcases get
heavier and heavier as she rises.*

SLIDE: THE SWITCHBOARD—Reception

*AUNT SHADIE walks towards small lights that fade up and
down. As she approaches, lights fade up on the back of
ROSE sitting at her switchboard. Her lobby is a 1960s hotel.
ROSE is dressed conservatively in 1960s attire. The
switchboard beeps and lights. She connects throughout.
AUNT SHADIE huffs herself forward.*

AUNT SHADIE:

Excuse me.

ROSE:

(*not looking at her*) Can I help you?

AUNT SHADIE:

Yeah sure. I'm looking for a place to leave my baggage
for a while.

ROSE:

I'm sorry, I can't do that.

AUNT SHADIE:

Why, because I'm In ...

ROSE:

... naked. Yes, that's it. You'll have to register first. I can't
be taking just anybody's baggage now, can I? Can you
write your name?

AUNT SHADIE:
Listen, I'm naked, not stupid.

ROSE:
Oh. Well, I'm just trying to help you people out.

AUNT SHADIE:
Why don't you look at me when you say that?

ROSE turns slowly around revealing a black eye and bruises on her face.

AUNT SHADIE:
Wow, they sure dragged you through it.

ROSE:
Humph. (*ROSE looks away from AUNT SHADIE's nakedness*)

AUNT SHADIE:
Haven't you ever seen anybody nude before?

ROSE:
Not up front.

AUNT SHADIE:
I'm not sure if I should feel sorry for you or not. Well, I went to bed wearing clothes, and then I woke up naked as a jailbird.

ROSE:
I woke up naked once.

AUNT SHADIE:
What, a million years ago?

ROSE:
Pardon me?

AUNT SHADIE:
I said, good for you.

ROSE:
> Aren't you cold?

AUNT SHADIE:
> Of course, I'm cold.

ROSE:
> Here, put this on.

> *ROSE takes a big beige cardigan from her chair and hands it to her.*

AUNT SHADIE:
> Now I feel ugly.

ROSE:
> It's from England.

AUNT SHADIE:
> Like I said, now I feel ugly.

ROSE:
> It's the same one the Queen wore on her inaugural visit to Canada.

AUNT SHADIE:
> Like I said, ugly. (*looking at the sweater*) Ugly. For a queen, you'd think she'd dress better. It's almost like she's punishing herself. If I had all her money, I wouldn't be wearing all those dowdy dresses. Just once I'd like her to wear a colour. Something not beige or plaid. Something blue maybe. Something that gives her colour: Red!

ROSE:
> Mothers of countries do not wear red.

AUNT SHADIE:
> She's a mother alright. Always did love those white gloves though. They remind me of white swans, especially when she waves. It's kinda pretty actually.

ROSE:
My mother always wore gloves. She used to say a lady wasn't a lady unless she wore gloves.

AUNT SHADIE:
Hmm. My mother wore mitts. They were white though, and furry. Big rabbit mitts. When my mother waved, it wasn't so much pretty as it was sad.

ROSE:
Waving can be sad.

AUNT SHADIE waves like a queen.

Where you going?

AUNT SHADIE:
I'm dying for a smoke.

ROSE:
What about registering?

ROSE watches as AUNT SHADIE signs her name.

Rita Louise James.

AUNT SHADIE:
There, you satisfied?

ROSE:
Just doing my job.

AUNT SHADIE:
What's that?

ROSE:
I'm taking account.

AUNT SHADIE:
Reminds me of the government. Taking count but not accountable.

She picks up her suitcases and begins to leave.

ROSE:

You're going like that?

AUNT SHADIE:

(*looks down on herself*) Why not?

ROSE:

You sure you don't want me to find you some pants?

AUNT SHADIE:

It's alright. There's a good draft ...

ROSE:

Oh please.

AUNT SHADIE:

... and frankly, if the pants look anything like the cardigan, I might as well be dead.

ROSE:

Suit yourself.

AUNT SHADIE:

I always have.

AUNT SHADIE keeps on walking. Lights fade on ROSE. AUNT SHADIE stops and sits on her suitcases. She reaches inside one of them and pulls out a pack of tobacco and rolls a cigarette. She reaches in and picks up an outfit from when she was a housewife. She smells the material and closes her eyes in memory. The clothes talk to her and she to them. She drapes them over her body and smokes her thinking smoke. Lights fade, leaving a bright butt and smoke rising up.

SLIDE: **Rose Doreen Holmes, 52, died January 27, 1965 with a 0.51 blood-alcohol reading. "Coroner's inquiry reported she was found nude on her bed and had recent bruises on her** *scalp, nose, lips and chin. There was no evidence of violence, or suspicion of foul play.* "

Lights fade up on ROSE, as she affectionately touches her switchboard. It responds with light flashes and beeps and muffled voices.

ROSE:

I've always been right here. No matter where I am, I am in between people connecting. I like to think I'm the one who connects them, but mostly I like to think that they have to go through me. If nothing else, it gives me a place. A place in the making, the flashes of being … the feeling of feeding that beeping energy into a whole that understands it, and soothes it, into a gentle darkness. A small whimper when it enters—a connection between the here and there—a giant light it becomes. It begins and ends with the beeping, but it goes through me. I wait for the cry like a mother listening, hoping to slot the right thing into its void—hoping to be the one to bring about the pure answer. Again, the pure gentle darkness that says I have listened and you were lovely, no matter how loud your beeping cry becomes, no matter how many times I wanted to help but couldn't. There is something maternal about it, the wanting to help, the trying, going through the motions on the switchboard, but in the end just being there always it seems just listening to voices looking for connection, an eternal connection between women's voices and worlds.

ROSE leans over and nosily watches AUNT SHADIE enter REBECCA's world.

Everybody always thinks that the switchboard operator is listening in on their conversations, and they're not always wrong. The tricky thing is to act like you don't know a thing. I swear on the Queen, it's a tricky thing.

AUNT SHADIE enters dressed as a young housewife. She is carrying her suitcases and a folded piece of paper. She sets the suitcases down and places a paper on the table. She turns to leave, but stops as REBECCA picks it up.

SLIDE: RUNNING SHOES

SFX: Sound of wind in the trees.

Backdrop gradually brings in close-ups of Hastings Street when it was the centre of shopping. The Army and Navy, Woolworth's—late 1960s/70s.

REBECCA:

My dad—the Character—was still full-limbed but hard-of-hearing when he died. Still asking "Eh?" after every sentence I spoke, but quick to hear the sound of change falling to the ground. Death was no big surprise for him. The thing he couldn't get out from under was the day she left. I found him holding a piece of paper she had put on the kitchen table. He held it for a long time and then simply folded it and put it in his pocket. "Where's Mom?" I asked.

SFX: Sound of tree falling and landing.

He said, "She went for a walk." I thought maybe she had gone to the IGA or something. Somebody was always having to go to the IGA. When she didn't return and he didn't move, I started complaining about the big fact that I was supposed to get new running shoes today. I was supposed to go downtown today. I was supposed to get a hamburger today ... milkshakes, fries and ketchup at Woolworth's. It was supposed to have been a great day, and now we had to wait. I was getting pissed off, because I was getting tired of going to the Salvation Army for smelly clothes, and I felt like I was gonna be normal like everyone else when Mom said we could go to the Army and Navy and get something new, something that smelled good, something that nobody had ever worn. Blue suede running shoes—three stripes on either side. I had to have them. It was unbearable, and my dad just standing there, and my mom deciding to go to the IGA. I thought it was a master plan. Both of them against me being normal. I started yelling—the injustice too great. My dad just stood there like he didn't hear anything. "Get in the truck," he said. We went. I ate hamburgers and floats and fries and everything I could see in the posters of food on the walls of the Woolworth's cafeteria on Hastings Street. We went to the Army and Navy. We went home. No Mom. Again. "Where's Mom?" again. He said, "She left us. I didn't know anything was wrong." He sat down. I took my running shoes off. I would never wear them again. Nothing was going to be normal.

REBECCA takes the running shoes off and kicks them. AUNT SHADIE turns around and silently picks them up, putting them properly under her chair. She exits.

Fade out.

SFX: Sound of car streams, transforming into the tide.

SLIDE: FOUR DAYS: DAY 1—Glenaird Hotel

SFX: Sound of tide hitting the edge of the island/bed.

The hotel room is an ocean of blue. The bed an island. The lone woman sits on her island. She is wet and holds a white pillow that shapes her different needs. The comfort of a child, a lover. THE WOMAN reaches over and grabs a drink from the table beside her. She places it down and in … in her own drinking rhythm. The ocean gets deeper in its colour.

Rhythms of a drinking room: 1) Tide—Time, 2) Light vs. Shadow, 3) Drinking Rhythm.

SFX: Sound of the tide begins to increase and finally sprays to telephone static.

SLIDE: I'M SCARED TO DIE 1

A click of light on. MAVIS sits in a huge beaten-up armchair. Her hotel room matches the chair. It is beaten and slightly tinged with hues of brown. As she sits, MAVIS leafs through her address book looking and reminiscing about each entry. She urgently picks up the phone and dials. A light flashes up on the switchboard, and we hear ROSE speak in the darkness.

MAVIS:

Hi, Mona? It's me.

SFX: Weird static and otherworldly connection.

ROSE:

I'm sorry, you've reached the operator.

MAVIS:

The operator? I didn't want any operator. I dialed the numbers myself. I'm more than capable of calling a long-distance number.

ROSE:

I'm sure you are. At any rate, you've reached the operator. (*very polite*) Can ... I ... help ... you?

MAVIS:

Well, I guess if you're just sitting on your ass you could put me through—save me the time of letting my fingers do the walking.

ROSE:

I'm sorry, I can't do that.

MAVIS:

Are you gonna help me or not?

ROSE:

Well, to be honest ... no one's ever reached me on the phone before, and I just don't know if it's house policy or not.

MAVIS:

What kind of house are you in where people call and you don't help them?

ROSE:

Don't raise your voice at me. I'm just following rules.

MAVIS:

Whose rules?

ROSE:

Management.

MAVIS:

(*covers the receiver with her hand*) Bitch!

ROSE:

Pardon me?

MAVIS:

I said, isn't that rich.

ROSE:

I'll put this call through just this once as a special favour, but this is highly unusual.

MAVIS:

Sure ... whatever.

SFX: Sound of real telephone connection.

(*ring*) Hi, Mona. I just thought ... (*ring*) ... got to thinking of you and thought I'd call. Actually, I just thought I'd call 'cause (*ring*) I wondered if you and Bill might be coming into town sometime. You know, change of scenery and all ... (*ring*) Doing good here, though (*ring*) just would be nice to hear your voice. I'll try back later, okay. (*ring*) We'll talk about all sorts of things. What I need is a good laugh. (*ring*) You know, a laugh so hard liquid comes from your nose like that time ... (*ring*) Well, anyways, here I am going on ... Just would be nice to talk about some old times maybe. (*ring*) I'd like that. I'd ... like ... that ...

She slowly places the receiver to her chest.

SFX: Sound of telephone ringing empty.

MAVIS looks back at her address book. Picks it up, and begins tracing names and thinking on each entry. Lights fade.

SFX: The telephone starts to buzz like a chainsaw under.

SLIDE: REBECCA—Hastings Street

The backdrop gives us a close-up of Pigeon Square. The buildings become smaller like stumps of logs. REBECCA sits at her table drinking. She holds a harmonica in her hand.

SFX: Sound of harmonica takes over the buzz of the chainsaw.

When she hears the sound of the harmonica, she gets up. A man enters and sits on one of the stumps. He watches her.

REBECCA:

I'm dancing in Pigeon Square. It's not a dream, it's a memory. I'm four years old, and I don't have to ask why they call it Pigeon Square. There's pigeon shit everywhere. At four a genius ... I know. A row of old men are sitting like stumps ... smoking, laughing, tilting their heads back in a chuckle or a slug of rum. They are talking to the Character—my dad. He's playing the harmonica. I'm pretending I'm a dancer. We don't know who's pretending more. Me, or him. But my feet are hitting the squares like I know what I'm doing, and he's hitting all the notes they can hear. They take their pennies out and splash them down around my dancing feet. The coppers fall ... it is the most beautiful sound you can imagine, because you see I am very special, and talented, and the "poor bastards," as my father would say, are happy, clapping. I bow. My dad takes my hand. We say goodbye. Some of them touch my cheek like they remember a daughter, some smile and wave a mitt, not a glove ...

The man finishes clapping, and reaches up to her ...

... and one reaches his glove to surround my braid. My dad—the Character—takes his hand and says to the man in the clearest logger "I could kill you": "Enough." The man lets go of my braid. My father, in the clearest "I love you," squishes my shoulder in a hug and says, "It's time to get the chain for the power saw. It should be fixed by now."

REBECCA turns back to the table and takes a drink. The man gets up and leaves.

It should be fixed by now.

SFX: Sound of rhythmic clapping echoes, and start of laughing.

SLIDE: THE BARBERSHOP QUARTET 1—Barbershop

SFX: The real sound of a man laughing drunkenly.

Lights up on the interior of a barbershop. It is old and worse for wear. Mirrors reflect back. MARILYN sits in one of the barber chairs, her back to us. Her hair flows over the back of the chair as the BARBER cleans and preps his utensils. He exits briefly. MARILYN looks closely into the mirror, as a reflection of herself as MARILYN À LA FARRAH FAWCETT looks back at her, becoming larger and more beautiful in the mirror. MARILYN À LA FARRAH FAWCETT begins to sing softly. She enjoys her hair dream. The BARBER enters dressed in hyper whites and drapes a white cape over her and her hair dream. He turns the barber light on, and it begins to slowly rotate—a red-and-white swirl. He places a bottle between her legs and tenderly begins to braid her hair in one long braid. He suddenly grabs her braid roughly and takes his scissors to cut it. She grabs it back in a tug of war.

MARILYN:
> Enough.

> *He leans over her and grabs the bottle. He brings it to her lips tenderly. She drinks. It spills.*

BARBER:
> Down the hatch, baby.
> Twenty bucks if you drink it right down.
> Down the hatch, baby.
> Right down—finish it right down.

> *She gulps and they laugh. He starts to twirl the barber chair faster and faster.*

> *Fade out.*

SLIDE: *ROOM 23, WHEN YOU'RE 33*—Clifton Hotel

Lights up on an old beat-up room. It is animated by an old DRESSER with an ugly personality. Small and battered, it has three drawers with a mirror on top. VALERIE stands in front of the mirror thinking about 23-year-old tits and adjusting her tits in her shirt.

THE DRESSER:
> You have a nice set.

VALERIE:
> Oh, shut up.

THE DRESSER:
> Really.

VALERIE:
> Why ... don't ... you ... shut up?

THE DRESSER:
> Why don't you make me?

VALERIE:
Just shut your drawers.

THE DRESSER:
Make me.

She takes her shirt off and is trying to get her bra off. It's stubborn.

VALERIE:
If I have to tell you again, you're gonna get it.

THE DRESSER:
Get what?

VALERIE:
A big fat punch in the chest.

THE DRESSER:
Valerie. Pick a drawer—any drawer.

THE DRESSER displays each drawer.

VALERIE:
Pick it yourself. Can't you see I'm busy here?

THE DRESSER:
Too busy to pick a drawer.

VALERIE:
Too busy to pick my nose.

THE DRESSER:
Too busy to pick your ass.

VALERIE:
Too busy to pick your ass.

They laugh.

THE DRESSER:
Pick a drawer.

VALERIE:
What do I get?

THE DRESSER:
What do you want?

VALERIE:
Nice lingerie.

THE DRESSER:
What colour?

VALERIE:
Red.

THE DRESSER:
What do I get?

VALERIE:
You get to watch me put it on.

THE DRESSER:
Maybe you're not my type.

VALERIE:
Eeeeee—an uppity dresser. I got a real problem if you're my type, don't I? What is your type, old squat one?

THE DRESSER:
A tall chest with two big knobs.

VALERIE:
You're a pig of a dresser.

THE DRESSER:
You're a pig.

VALERIE:
Come over here and say that.

THE DRESSER:
You come over here and say that.

VALERIE:
Pig!

THE DRESSER:
Whore!

VALERIE:
I'll knock your drawers off.

THE DRESSER:
Why don't you just get my drawers off?

VALERIE:
That's no way to talk to a lady.

THE DRESSER:
What lady? I don't see any LAY-DEE.

The mirror of THE DRESSER starts to reflect a man's face.

VALERIE:
And I don't see any-BODY. So shut up!

THE DRESSER:
Okay, baby. Okay. Do you want to see what's in my drawers?

VALERIE:
Probably skid marks.

THE DRESSER:
Come on, baby ... take a peek. Come on, baby. That's it, baby.

She draws closer to the top drawer. It slides open slowly. She leans over to look in. A hand comes out and squeezes her tit.

VALERIE:

Fuckin' pig !

THE DRESSER:

Let go! You fuckin' whore!

She squeezes the drawer on his hand.

VALERIE:

Say Valerie is the prettiest one of them all.

THE DRESSER:

Val-er-ie is the pretti-est? ... CHUG of them all.

VALERIE:

That's a bad dresser.

She squeezes the drawer harder on his hand.

He screams.

THE DRESSER:

Valerie is the prettiest lay-dee of them all.

VALERIE:

And smart.

THE DRESSER:

... And smart.

VALERIE:

And she still has a great set of tits.

THE DRESSER:

... And she still has a great set of tits.

*She lets go of his hand, and it shrinks back into the drawer.
She turns.*

VALERIE:

I had two sons, you know ... and I still have great tits.

THE DRESSER:
Yah, you're a regular Hollywood dairy cow.

VALERIE:
What did you say?

THE DRESSER:
I said, you're a real Pocahontas.

VALERIE:
Fuck you.

THE DRESSER:
WHORE!

VALERIE:
PIG!

She kicks him in the drawers. He groans. He moves towards her, they wrestle, and fall on the floor wrestling. Fade out.

SFX: Sound of the tide. A slower rhythm.

SLIDE: FOUR DAYS: DAY 2—Glenaird Hotel— Continued.

It is dark. THE WOMAN stands on her bed/island and clicks on the light hanging from the ceiling. A pillow is propped up like a person next to her. The light of the light bulb sways slowly, back and forth. As she listens, she lifts the drink to her mouth and places it down slowly in her drinking rhythm. Repeats gesture, listening.

SFX: VOICE OVER—a fatherly male voice.

"Once upon a time, a very long time ago, there was a deer who lost its mother, because someone shot its mother. Something like the story of Bambi, except that the little fawn was adopted by a human family that loved it. And then someone said that the fawn that grew to a deer should be with its own kind, so the father of the human family, who

lived on the mainland, took a ferry and dropped the deer on an island miles away and hoped it would be happier. Well, the deer wasn't happy without the only family it had ever known, and it swam all the way back to its human family, and everything was going great, everything was going great, until it ate some lettuce from the neighbour's garden, and the neighbour shot it dead."

Rhythms of a drinking room: 1) Tide—Time, 2) Light vs. Shadow, 3) Drinking Rhythm, 4) Conversations—recent and past.

The hanging light stills. Fade out.

SFX: Sound of tide blends into the electronic sound of static.

SLIDE: *I'M SCARED TO DIE 2*

Lights fade up on MAVIS sitting in her chair. She sits in the exact same spot and manner. She is leafing through her address book. She finds a name and stops and smiles. Slowly, she runs her hand over herself, not so much sexually but as if remembering sex. She picks up the phone and dials him. Lights fade up on ROSE's switchboard.

MAVIS:

Hello, John … it's me.

ROSE:

It's me, Rose—your operator. What number were you calling?

MAVIS:

This is an emergency, if you have to know. Big Nose.

ROSE:

You don't have to be rude—I was just trying to be helpful. I have a very demanding job, and I don't need this static from you …

MAVIS:

Well, I have a lot better things to do than talking to people I didn't want to talk to.

ROSE:

Listen, madam.

MAVIS:

Don't use that tone with me.

ROSE:

Don't think that all I do all day is sit on my big fanny and wait for people to talk to me like this—people who have no appreciation for the fine art of communication.

MAVIS:

It gets pretty damn bad when you can't even make a phone call without having a conversation with someone you don't want to talk to. Nose.

ROSE:

And about that nose business. I don't have a big nose. If the facts be known, I have quite a fine upturned nose, and if you're referring to the fact that I asked you who you were calling—well, that has nothing to do with nosiness and everything to do with ...

MAVIS:

I'm asking you for nothing—but for you—to *shut up*— and put me through to who I need to talk to—and not have to go through—this talk ... talk ... talk. Cluck ... Cluck ... Cluck ...

ROSE:

Practicality, every time I pick up the phone ...

MAVIS:

... like a goddamn BEAKY chicken!

A long, hurt silence.

ROSE:

I'll thank you very much to refrain from making comments about my features.

MAVIS:

Don't think that just because you use bigger words than me and you went to reception school or something, that makes you better than me.

ROSE:

I'm just doing my job, and that's all you can ask out of anybody—that a person do the job they were meant to do, and I try to do my job a million times a day.

MAVIS:

Like you know it all, when you don't know me and you don't give a damn how I'm feeling or what I'm worried about or why I can't get off my ass and just leave my room.

ROSE:

… A million times a day.

MAVIS:

I'm so scared I can't move.

ROSE:

… A million times a day …

MAVIS:

I can't breathe.

ROSE:

I get this static a million times a day …

MAVIS:

I listen.

ROSE:

… times a day …

MAVIS:

 I cry.

ROSE:

 … from the static of nothing.

MAVIS:

 A million times a day.

ROSE:

 I want …

MAVIS:

 I reach out for it.

ROSE:

 … and nothing.

> *ROSE plugs her through. A surprising click for everyone.*

> *SFX: VOICE OVER—"I'm sorry, the number you have reached
>   has been disconnected. Please call your operator … "*

> *MAVIS tries to talk over the recording as if nothing is wrong.*

MAVIS:

Hey, John. It's me. Remember me? Mavis. Mavis Gertrude
Jones. Played baseball real good. You know, you used to
say I had the best arm on the team. You know, you used
to say I was the smartest person you'd ever met, because
I was always reading those Britannica Encyclopedias with
the letters on them. You used to say I had the best body
in town—just kidding … and a pretty good bannock
maker too. The queen of bannock making.

> *SFX: VOICE OVER—"I'm sorry, the number you have reached
>   has been disconnected. Please call your operator and … "*

I miss your smile. I remembered your smile the other
day. Going into a piece of that bread and coming out all
greasy, with butter and lard—all sassy. You could always

make me smile ... make me feel safe with those big brown arms of yours. John? Anyways, I remembered those big arms of yours, and I was thinking I'd really like to borrow them for a few weeks. I know, that seems silly, but I'd really like to have that feeling with me right now. Just until I can get away from *this* feeling. Shake it away with your big arms wrapped right around me. John? John.

Arms of the brown armchair extend like real arms and curl around her. She hugs them and love-coos in comfort.

Thank you, John. You always were sweet to me. Sweet Johnnie.

She love-coos to herself and Johnnie's arms, and finally falls asleep.

SFX: Soft sound of pigeons cooing grows underneath.

Pigeon wings mix and blur and land on the backdrop behind. AUNT SHADIE slowly emerges from them and walks towards REBECCA's table. She sits down silently.

SLIDE: WHITE BIRDS—Hastings Street

The huge "W" of the Woodward's building is brightly lit neon red and appears above it all.

REBECCA:

My mother. I see her in half-looks everywhere. I call it seeing-the-white-bird look. This white is not the colour of skin, but the flutter of hope. Women's white birds. Sometimes you witness it, and it makes you cry. Sometimes I see it across a coupled room, and when I do see it—I see my mother's chin bending down limp to her chest.

A young AUNT SHADIE's chin drops down to her chest. REBECCA looks in her direction.

Not to look at me, though the crease in her neck makes it possible for her to look at me, with tenderness, or to look at her man with tenderness, or to look at anything smaller than her, with tenderness. But to bend that long neck down, till her beak reaches her collar bone, and sits for a long time before it comes up. It sits so long, you ask: "What's wrong, Mom? What's wrong?"

AUNT SHADIE doesn't answer.

So long that your heart starts to beat, because something is wrong, so wrong, and nobody will speak. Not your dad—the Character—who spoke words and made this bird-killing silence ... And finally, she lifts her head ... finally she lifts her head, but something is gone. Something dead sits in her eyes, and rests itself on the tone of her voice, when my dad—the Character—asks, irritated: "Jesus, Rita. What's wrong now?"

AUNT SHADIE raises her chin slowly. Smiles faintly.

She slowly smiles oddly. "Nothing." My dad—the Character—continues talking, as if nothing has died. But I saw it flutter and die. "Are you alright, Mom? Mom?"

AUNT SHADIE rises and slowly walks away.

She is silent, and gets up and walks to the washroom, or we leave the restaurant, or she goes to the other room, and that hope dies without him even knowing it had anything to do with him. A man kills enough. A woman keeps on walking.

REBECCA gets up and watches her leave.

SLIDE: SWITCHBOARD—Reception

Lights up on AUNT SHADIE as she arrives at the reception counter. She is putting trapper clothes over her young housewife clothes. She leans on the reception counter, putting on a parka and rabbit mitts. ROSE's face is no longer bruised. AUNT SHADIE lays the sweater on the desk.

AUNT SHADIE:
Thanks for the sweater.

ROSE:
You're welcome, Rita.

AUNT SHADIE:
You're welcome, Rose. Call me Aunt Shadie. Everybody else does.

ROSE:
Alright, Aunt Shadie. Where did you get the clothes?

AUNT SHADIE:
I found them in my baggage.

AUNT SHADIE begins to leave.

ROSE:
Nice gloves.

AUNT SHADIE:
Mitts.

She looks proudly at her mitts.

I used to be a real good trapper when I was young. You wouldn't believe it now that I'm such a city girl, but before when my legs and body were young and muscular, I could go forever. Walking those traplines with snowshoes. The sun coming down sprinkling everything with crystals, some floating down, and dusting that white comforter with magic. I would walk that trapline like a map, knowing every turn, every tree, every curve the land uses to confuse us. I felt like I was part of the magic, that wasn't confused. The crystals sticking to the cold, and the cold sticking to my black hair, my eyebrows, my clothes, my breath. A trap set. An animal caught.

Red. If it squirmed, I would take my rifle and shoot it as fast as I could. Poor thing. I hate to see an animal suffer. Meegwetch, and thank you.

ROSE:

It sounds barbaric.

AUNT SHADIE:

Shopping at the Woodward's food floor is barbaric. You never know what you are eating. Even if it says ground hamburger meat on the package, how do you know it *is* ground hamburger? What is ground *ham*-burger? And why do they have to grind it? Everybody just eats it. No one questions where it came from. Must be the big hamburger animal. That big "W" in the sky doesn't stand for Woodward's, but for "what." WHAT did I just eat?

ROSE takes out a pair of long, white gloves and puts them on.

ROSE:

I like that swan metaphor.

AUNT SHADIE:

The what for? Swans are the great hamburger animal?

ROSE:

Don't be silly. Gloves look like swans.

AUNT SHADIE:

Well, actually, if I was to really think about it … probably more like skinned rabbit mitts.

ROSE:

I like the swans.

AUNT SHADIE:

Did you ever feel like hugging a swan?

ROSE:

Yes, I have.

AUNT SHADIE:

> You? You have hugged a swan.

ROSE:

> Yes, I have. I have an appreciation for animals too, you know.

AUNT SHADIE:

> No, I mean. I'm sure you do in your own polite way, but ... a swan.

ROSE:

> It felt good.

AUNT SHADIE:

> You got me kinda worried here. What kind of hug was it?

ROSE:

> Just a quick peck on the cheek. But it wasn't a kiss. I just walked up to it real quiet, foot by foot, and placed my arms around it just for a second. Nice swan.

AUNT SHADIE:

> Have you ever hugged a swan so much you almost squished it?

ROSE:

> No, I haven't actually. What kind of animal lover do you think I am?

AUNT SHADIE:

> Every time I see a swan, I feel like hugging it hard. The kind of hug where you just can't stand how much you love it, or feel for it, and you're hugging and hugging it, and you just get carried away.

ROSE:

> How many swans have you hugged?

AUNT SHADIE:

I never hugged a swan. I just figured anything that beautiful wouldn't want to be hugged. My nephews ... yes ... my daughter when she was small, my parents when they were old, my pillow when I was lonely ... myself when I was stupid.

ROSE:

How many things have you squished while hugging?

AUNT SHADIE:

I never really squished anything. I was just trying to get across to you that feeling of loving something so much you could squish it. I think everybody should have that feeling at least once.

ROSE:

Hugging till you squish, or being squished?

AUNT SHADIE:

Both. But ...

ROSE:

What?

AUNT SHADIE:

It makes you kinda want to be the squished one, doesn't it?

ROSE:

Yes ... yes, it does actually. Tea?

AUNT SHADIE:

Sure.

> *REBECCA moves from her table and slots some coins into the juke box.*
>
> **SLIDE: FOUR DAYS: DAY 3—Glenaird Hotel— Continued.**

As the lyrics of the song fade, the music remains under. She waltzes to it and to the VOICE OVER of a conversation.

SFX: Sound of the tide fades up and eventually takes over.

SFX: In a convincing male voice, like music ...

SFX: "You move so beautifully." (she steps)

THE WOMAN:

Thank you. (*she stumbles*)

SFX: "You have the most beautiful brown skin." (she steps)

Thank you. (*she stumbles*)

SFX: "You don't have to be scared. I would never let anybody hurt you."

She steps and loses her balance. She takes her face out of her pillow's shoulder and looks down. She looks down at her legs as if something is wrong with them. The silhouette of a deer's legs and hooves looks back from the floor. She begins to cry, confused. The pillow becomes a MAN, dressed like a pillow. He lifts her chin slowly, and dries her tears. Lights out.

Rhythms of a drinking room: 1) Tide—Time, 2) Lights vs. Shadow, 3) Drinking Rhythm, 4) Conversations—recent and past, 5) Music/Movement—romantic.

SFX: The phone rings.

SLIDE: I'M SCARED TO DIE 3

MAVIS wakes in a start and picks up the phone.

MAVIS:

It's okay, Johnnie ... it's probably just my operator. You need your rest. Hello, who is it?

ROSE:

It's Rose.

MAVIS:

Rose who?

ROSE:

Rose—you know very well, Rose who.

MAVIS:

What do you want?

ROSE:

I thought I'd call and check in with you. I heard somebody breathing funny on your line.

MAVIS:

I just got company that's all.

ROSE:

What kind of company?

MAVIS:

Man company. He just kinda showed up out of the brown.

ROSE:

Humph. I never did trust a man that just showed up.

MAVIS:

Well, some of my best romances came from men that just showed up.

ROSE:

Suit yourself … as long as nothing is wrong.

MAVIS:

Listen, Rose, I appreciate your worry. It's just been nice and peaceful for a change. I just been having a creepy feeling, and that's why I don't go out much. But with John here it's not so bad.

ROSE:

What kind of creepy feeling?

MAVIS:

> (*softly*) Death.

ROSE:

> Mavis, I can't hear you when you talk soft like that.

MAVIS:

> (*louder*) Nothing.

ROSE:

> Mavis, I think there's ...

MAVIS:

> My sister. It's my sister.

ROSE:

> You're scared of your sister?

MAVIS:

> Isn't everyone?

ROSE:

> Why don't you talk to her? I'm not doing anything anyway.

MAVIS:

> Sure. I'll be brave. (*she adjusts herself*) Put me through, Rose. Meegweetch.

ROSE:

> Fine, just put me through ... no, thank you ... no, that's great of you, Rose ... thanks for taking the time to ... Well, McWitch to you too!

MAVIS:

> Meegweetch, Rose. Meegweetch. It means "Thank you."

> *Click of call going through. It rings and ...*

> Hi, Laverne. It's me ... Ma ...

> *SFX: Answering machine.*

"Hi. You've reached Laverne ... "

Laverne?

"We're not in right now, but if you leave a message we'll get back to you as soon as possible, or you can reach us on the pager at (204) 266-4325, or fax us at (204) 266-5646, or at work at (204) 456-1425, or just leave a message after the beep, I guess."

Gawd. Hi ... it's me. Mavis ... your sister. Yeah, it's been a long time, but I was thinking of you and ... I'm doing real good. I just thought I'd call and say ... it's good to hear your voice, even if it's on the answering machine. It sounds like you got a lot of stuff ... Laverne. You know when someone wants your chair, your place? Not like our mother, or an elder, or someone we know, but when someone you don't like wants your place, and you can feel them thinking about it ... just waiting for you to get up ... concentrating on your getting up so they can jump in your place, and never give it back. I can feel someone getting closer and closer, inch by inch, stepping closer, and pretty soon they'll be in my seat. Breathing where I should be sitting. I know that sounds weird, but it's just a feeling.

SFX: Answering machine clicks off.

ROSE:

I wouldn't call if I'd been drinking or anything. I love you ... I didn't mean to sound stupid.

SLIDE: THE BARBERSHOP QUARTET 2— Barbershop

SFX: The sound of MARILYN singing softly.

The interior of the barbershop flares up. The red-and-white swirl of the barber light is twirling. PENNY sits drunkenly in the barber chair as a beautiful MARILYN À LA FARRAH FAWCETT emerges. Reaching her hands out to PENNY, she begins to clear PENNY's hair from her face gently. PENNY looks into the mirror and sees herself as PENNY À LA PAT BENETAR. They both laugh. The BARBER enters dressed in hyper barber white. He places a white cape over PENNY and her hair dream. The BARBER takes the bottle and places it between her legs and begins to braid her hair in one long braid. MARILYN's song gets strained as she reaches for the bottle in an effort to take it from them. The BARBER grabs it and raises it to PENNY's lips seductively. He moves to climb on top of her.

BARBER:

Down the hatch, baby.
Twenty bucks if you drink it right down.
Down the hatch, baby.
Drink it right down.

Fade out.

SLIDE: KEEP ON WALKING—Hastings Street

Lights up below on REBECCA as she walks. Backdrop of Hastings Street. Signs in windows advertising for HELP. AUNT SHADIE's face appears in the images.

REBECCA:

Where do women walk to when they have fallen? Sure, you could say some of them walk on to something better. They leave their bastardly husbands, get a job and free themselves from suffocating domesticality. They learn to type, or waitress, or become your chambermaid, your housekeeper, your cleaner, your babysitter and pretty soon it feels like this new-found freedom is not so free— the man's face has just changed. If they can stand this, they stay. If not, one day they just keep walking.

SLIDE: THE WRONG ROOM—Balmoral Hotel

VERNA:

… One fuckin' day at a time.

Lights up on VERNA sitting on her bed in the hotel room. A bottle of wine sits on the bedside table eyeing her. She fondles the bottle, wanting to take a drink but touches a toy plane in her lap instead. She talks to her ex-husband on the phone ...

Yeah. I'm serious. I got a gift for him ... for his birthday. If you come and pick me up ... maybe we could take the kid for Chinese food, and I could give him his present then. Yeah, I'll be downstairs out in front waiting. I'll be down there ... I told you.

SLIDE: ROOM 23, WHEN YOU'RE 33—Clifton Hotel

The room is dishevelled. VALERIE is lying on the floor, THE DRESSER is lying on the floor. They are both trying to get themselves back together.

THE DRESSER:
You have a nice set.

VALERIE:
Oh, shut up.

THE DRESSER:
Really.

VALERIE:
Why don't you shut up?

THE DRESSER:
Why don't you make me?

VALERIE:
I made you already.

THE DRESSER:
I made *you* already.

VALERIE:
No reason to be a sore loser.

THE DRESSER:
Pick a drawer.

VALERIE:
Go away.

THE DRESSER:
Go on, pick a drawer. I'll bet you'll like this drawer.

His bottom drawer slides open. The TOMMY drawer speaks.

SFX: Voices of her two sons.

TOMMY:
Mommy?

VALERIE:
Tomm ...

TOMMY:
Mommy.

VALERIE:
Tommy.

TOMMY:
Hey, Mom.

VALERIE:
Hey, Tom. Tom ... what are you doing in there?

TOMMY:
Mom, I'm a real good dancer now. I can even dance better than Evan.

His second drawer opens. The EVAN drawer.

EVAN:
Yeah, right.

TOMMY:
I can.

EVAN:
Like hell!

VALERIE:
Don't swear.

EVAN:
Don't tell me what to do.

VALERIE:
I'm your mother.

EVAN:
Yeah, right.

VALERIE:
How are things?

TOMMY:
Good.

EVAN:
How do you think things are?

TOMMY:
When are you coming home?

EVAN:
Probably never.

VALERIE:
Soon … real soon.

EVAN:
Soon … liar.

TOMMY:
When are you coming home? It's been a long time now.

VALERIE:
It's hard to come right now. But soon. I'm gonna get this job and soon …

TOMMY:
How soon?

EVAN:
Soon. Liar.

TOMMY:
How long is soon?

VALERIE:
I can picture you in my head.

EVAN:
Take a picture—it lasts longer.

VALERIE:
Maybe, I could take a couple days off …

EVAN:
… drinking.

VALERIE:
… working. And we could get together …

EVAN:
Soon.

VALERIE:
Just me, and my two little men.

TOMMY:
Mom?

EVAN:
Mom?

VALERIE:
Yeah?

The drawers don't respond. She gets real close to the drawers.

Yeah, I'm listening. I'm right here. I'M RIGHT HERE.

THE DRESSER:
Yeah. Here you go, bitch!

The dresser lets her have it with the drawers. One of the drawers slams her head, the other her stomach and legs—it buckles her. It keeps punching her till she lays on the floor semi-conscious.

THE DRESSER slowly opens the TOMMY drawer.

TOMMY:
Mommy?

She barely wakes.

VALERIE:
I'm coming … I'm coming.

She crawls to THE DRESSER. The top drawer slams her in the head. She slumps down, her head on the TOMMY drawer.

THE DRESSER's hand comes out of the top drawer and reaches down across her chest fondling her breasts. Lights out.

SLIDE: **Valerie Nancy Homes, 33. Died November 19, 1986 with a 0.04 blood-alcohol reading. "Jordan arrived at the Vancouver police station with his lawyer to report the death. He said he and Homes had been drinking for two days."**

SLIDE: **FOUR DAYS: DAY 4—Glenaird Hotel—Continued.**

SFX: Sound of the tide starts under. The slowest rhythm. The distorted sound of love whispers between a man and a woman.

The light bulb fades up slowly on the ocean that has become the room. THE WOMAN is lying flat on her bed. A pillow lies on top of her. Her hand over the side of the bed holds a drink. She drinks and floats, making a slow swimming motion with her pelvis.

SFX: VOICE OVER—A fatherly male voice—faster, more emotional.

"Someone had told her a story, a very, very long time ago, about a deer who lost its mother, because someone shot its mother. Something like the story of Bambi, except that the little fawn was adopted by a white family that loved it, and then someone said that the fawn that grew to be an Indian girl should be with its own kind, so the father of the white family, who lived on the mainland, took a ferry and dropped the Indian girl on an island miles away, and hoped she would be happier. Well, the Indian girl wasn't happy without the only family she had ever known, and she swam all the way back to her white family, and everything was going great ... everything was ... going ... great ..."

The pillow on top of her becomes the MAN DRESSED AS A PILLOW. He grinds into her, adding a violence to the swimming sex rhythm. She is totally disconnected to what is happening, staring straight up to the story.

THE WOMAN:
    ... Every thing was going great, until she decided that she really didn't belong anywhere. So she decided it would be better to surrender to the ocean, to just let go, than to swim so hard, for so long, just to get to the mainland and be shot by a neighbour over a head of lettuce. (*she laughs*)

Blackout.

SFX: Sound of the glass hitting the floor.

Rhythms of a drinking room: 1) Tide—Time, 2) Light vs. Dark, 3) Drinking rhythm, 4) Conversations—recent and past, 5) Music-Movement—romantic, 6) Sex.

Lights fade.

SLIDE: THE BARBERSHOP QUARTET 3— Barbershop

SFX: Sound of MARILYN and PENNY singing softly.

The interior of the barbershop flares up. The red-and-white swirl of the barbershop light is circling. MARILYN À LA FARRAH FAWCETT and PENNY À LA PAT BENATAR reflect out towards PATSY as she falls from the chair and begins to crawl away. The BARBER dressed in whites follows after her with the scissors. The scissors make a chopping noise as he grabs her braid. The red-and-white swirl of light intensifies the struggle. The song of MARILYN and PENNY intensifies as they call to her.

BARBER:
Down the hatch, baby.
Twenty bucks.if you drink it right down.
Down the hatch, baby.
Right down. Finish it right down.
Down the hatch, baby.
DRINK IT—DROWN.

The BARBER emerges from the swirl with Patsy's braid. He covers her body on the floor with his white cape. He turns and leaves, as THE WOMEN's reflections in the mirror begin to multiply and become surreal.

SLIDE: KEEP ON WALKING—Hastings Street— Continued.

The backdrop of windows of the hotel buildings. AUNT SHADIE's face appears in and out of the images.

REBECCA:

One might walk here. One story among a rooming house full of walking stories. I've come to find her story. My mother. My mother's one story. I walk through these streets. I walk through the women standing on legs like stilts. No pantyhose, but varicose seams everywhere, blue and yellow on their plastic skin. Skirts hiked up and shirts hiked down, their faces hollowed to a pout.

SLIDE: THE WRONG ROOM—Balmoral Hotel— Continued.

VERNA:

I'll be down there—I told you. Okay, thirty minutes. Yes—I said thirty minutes. Right out in front. THIR-TEE minutes.

She hangs up.

Ree-tard.

She starts talking to the plane.

My son'll like you. Almost spent my whole skinny cheque. I hope he likes you. I hope he likes me. I hope he's not mad. My son has a temper just like his mother.

The plane lifts from her hand, and its wings wave a "yes." VERNA laughs. She takes the plane and opens the door to go out. She forgets her purse and lets the plane idle.

SFX: Buzz of plane flying.

You stay here.

She turns to get her purse, and the plane is flying down the hallway. She calls to it.

It's not like you have to hold my hand—just wait up for me, will yah?

She loses sight of the plane as it descends the stairwell. She follows it a flight behind. Floor 7.

SFX: Sound of plane descending.

SFX: A slight whispering. A male voice that grows louder under and ...

"Can I get you a drink?" *(Continued)*

SLIDE: *I'M SCARED TO DIE 4*

Lights up on MAVIS sitting in her chair with John's arms wrapped around her tightly.

SFX: Sound of phone ringing.

MAVIS picks it up.

MAVIS:
Rose?

Lights up on ROSE plugging into MAVIS's line but getting a busy signal.

SFX: VOICE OVER—The phone beeps an aggressive, electronic:

"Can—I—get—you—a—drink?"

Lights down on ROSE.

MALE VOICE:
No. It's downstairs. I can't seem to transfer a call to you. She says she's your sister. Do you want to come and take it down here?

MAVIS:
Laverne? My sister.

MALE VOICE:
Do you want to come and take it down here?

MAVIS:

>(*puts her hand over the receiver*) My chair? Laverne. My chair? Laverne. Aahhh shit, I was just getting comfy. Okay, I guess I'll be right down.

>*She gently kisses Johnnie's arms and moves them gently to the side. She looks suspiciously around the room and murmurs under her breath.*

You even think of sitting in my chair and I'll kick your ass.

>*She drops the receiver and runs for the door and exits.*

>*SFX: Sound of quick footsteps down a flight of stairs.*

(*offstage*) Laverne? Goddamn it! (*slams phone*)

>*SFX: Sound of quicker steps up a flight of stairs.*

(*mumbling up*) My sister ... my ass ...

>*She emerges in the doorway. Her chair has been turned around to face her. A MAN sits in it.*

Get out of my chair!

MAN:

>Can I get you a drink?

MAVIS:

>Where is John?

MAN:

>John who?

>*SFX: Voice Over—Sound of static from the receiver and ...*

>*"If you need help, just hang up and dial your operator ... if you need help, just hang up and dial your operator."*

>*Lights fade.*

SLIDE: Mavis Gertrude Jones, 42. Died November 30, 1980 with a 0.34 blood-alcohol reading. An inquiry concluded Jones's death was "unnatural and accidental."

VERNA follows the plane down floor 6.

SFX: Descent of plane.

SFX: Louder. A male voice that grows louder and louder ...

"Can I get you a drink?" (Continued)

SLIDE: KEEP ON WALKING—Hastings Street—Continued.

Backdrop of close-up of grocery store. Faces / bottles. AUNT SHADIE's face appears and disappears.

REBECCA:

I walk through the elderly and the mentally ill and people stir-fried on Chinese cooking wine. I walk, and when I get tired I stop for a pack of smokes at the corner store and look at the Aqua Velva people in front of me in line. They are not blue. I then look at the Aqua Velva bottles all lined up pretty on the shelf next to the Aspirin. The most normal of refreshments to sell. I look into the woman punching the figures into the till. She could be my mother except that she is Asian. I look for some kind of clue that allows a hard-working woman who's worked hard all her life to ring up a bottle of Aqua Velva and sell it to an old man who is not "The Aqua Velva Man" but "Man with Huge Red Nose." She rings it in, all business, no trace of remorse. She stocks it for him—refreshment meeting cologne. Seller meeting buyer. It stinks, and I need a drink that isn't blue.

REBECCA exits.

AUNT SHADIE stands in front of the barbershop mirror. Three slides emerge, and three women stand behind the images of their slides. They begin to emerge from the barbershop mirror as AUNT SHADIE calls to them in song and they respond, in song, in rounds of their original languages.

THE WOMEN in the barbershop call to each fallen woman, in each solitary room. THE WOMEN respond and join them in song and ritual as they gather their voice, language and selves in the barbershop.

Throughout, the song floats in and out of each scene, submerging under some, and taking over others, flowing like a river. Each call and response a current. It grows in strength and intensity to the end of Act 1 where all their voices join force.

AUNT SHADIE:

Do I hear you sister like yesterday today
Ke-peh-tat-in/jee/ne-gee-metch
Das-goots/o-tahg-gos-ehk
Ahnotes/ka-kee-se-khak

> **SLIDE: Marilyn Wiles, 40. Died December 04, 1984 with a 0.51 blood-alcohol reading. An inquiry at the time concluded Wiles's death was "unnatural and accidental."**
>
> **Patsy Rosemary Forest, 25. Died July 03, 1982 with a 0.43 blood-alcohol reading. At the time of her death, the coroner said there was no indication of foul play.**
>
> **Penny Florence Ways, 45. Died June 08, 1985 with a 0.79 blood-alcohol reading. The coroner concluded her death was "unnatural and accidental."**

VERNA follows the plane down floor 5.

SFX: Descent of plane.

SFX: Louder. A male voice that grows louder under and ...

"Can I get you a drink?" (Continued)

Lights dimly up on VIOLET.

"Can I get you a drink?"(Continued)

THE WOMEN:
Do I hear you sister like yesterday today
Ke-peh-tat-in/jee/ne-gee-metch
Das-goots/o-tahg-gos-ehk
Ahnotes/ka-kee-se-khak

Under water—under time
Ee-tam-pehg/eetam-ehg
Te-pi-he-gun

SLIDE: VIOLET—Niagara Hotel

VIOLET, as she sits on the floor of her hotel room. Her focus upwards. The shadow of a man casts itself long on the walls. Her face reaches him mid-groin.

VIOLET:
I've swallowed it all. I've swallowed it all ... downtown, right between my lips. I didn't know if it was the neck of the bottle I was swallowing or his penis. Both have that musty kind of smell at the opening of it. Like it has been around for a while, waiting for the next set of lips but not cleaning in between deaths. Musty—you never know where it's been. I swallowed. Man's fingers weaved in my hair pulling down and up, down and up, down and up so many times I didn't know if it was the salt that filled me or the sting of the vodka. I don't even drink usually.

VIOLET's head falls down.

SLIDE: Violet Leslie Taylor, 27. Died October 12, 1987 with a 0.91 blood-alcohol reading. "She had

the highest blood-alcohol reading of all the women." No coroner's report has been issued.

THE WOMEN:
Do I hear you sister like yesterday today
Ke-peh-tat-in/jee/ne-gee-metch
Das-goots/o-tahg-gos-ehk
Ahnotes/ka-kee-se-khak

Hear your words right next to mine
Ee-pee-ta-man/ke-ta-yaur-e
Win/me-too-nee/o-ta

> *VERNA follows the plane down floor 4.*

> *SFX: Descent of plane.*

> *SFX: "Can I get you a drink?"*

THE WOMEN:
Do I hear you sister like yesterday today
Ke-peh-tat-in/jee/ne-gee-metch
Das-goots/o-tahg-gos-ehk
Ahnotes/ka-kee-se-khak

> **SLIDE: FOUR DAYS: THERE IS NO DAY FIVE—Glenaird Hotel—Continued.**

SFX: No sound.

The light bulb fades up. No movement. THE WOMAN lies flat on her bed, alone in the hotel room. Clothes up when they should be down. No pillow. The light becomes brighter and brighter revealing an ocean floor in low tide.

Light clicks out.

Rhythms of a drinking room: None.

THE WOMEN:
You are not speaking and yet I touch your words
Ee-ka/ee-I-am-e-en/maga-e-tagh-in-a-man/ke-ta
Ya-mi-win

> *SLIDE: Brenda A. Moore, 27. Died September 11, 1981*
> *with a 0.43 blood-alcohol reading. Coroner's*
> *report concluded her death was "unnatural*
> *and accidental."*

> *VERNA is on floor 3. She stops and listens for the buzz of the*
> *plane. Nothing but the sound of a man's voice coming from*
> *room 315. VERNA approaches it slowly.*

> *SFX: "Can I get you a drink? Can I get you a drink—a*
> *drink? Can I get you a drink?"*

THE WOMEN:
So the river says to me drink me feel better
Kwa-ne-ka-isit-/se-pe-h
Me-knee-qua-sin/me-thwa-ya

Like the river must've said to you first
Tas-koch-e-to-key/ka-key-e
Tisk/ne-s-tum

> *Below lights up on REBECCA as she sits at a table in the*
> *Empress Hotel.*

> *VERNA enters room 315. The man dressed as an airline*
> *pilot seats her. Her son's plane buzzes around her head as he*
> *hands her a drink.*

THE PILOT:
Can I get you a drink?

> *REBECCA looks up from her small, red, terry-clothed table.*
> *She motions two glasses.*

> *SFX: The plane sputters and sputters and smashes to the*
> *ground.*

Lights out.

*SLIDE: **Verna Deborah Gregory, 38. Died September 25, 1986 with a 0.63 blood-alcohol reading. Gregory's death was ruled "accidental as a result of acute alcohol poisoning."***

THE WOMEN:

Drink me—feel better
Me-knee-qua-sin/me-thwa-ya

There is no sadness just the war of a great thirst
Moi-ch/ke-qua-eh/ka-quat-ta-keye-ta-mo-win

*SLIDE: **VIOLET—Niagara Hotel—Continued.***

Lights fade dimly up on VIOLET as she detaches from her shadow. She leaves herself there with the man. She becomes smaller and more childlike, as she backs away and finally sits back on a swing and just stares, watching her woman self there with the man. Her body begins to become purple as AUNT SHADIE moves tenderly behind her and begins to swing her.

VIOLET:

It was the back and forth of it. Like being on a swing when I was a girl. My father pushing the swing into the sky. Back and forth, that's where my mind went from the past and up from the past and up and up ... I thought if I got any higher the swing would wrap around the pole and I would choke, but I went up after the last push, and after the last ... my legs pumping the air for flight.

THE WOMEN:

Do I see you sisters like yesterday today
Ke-peh-tat-in/jee/ne-gee-metch
Das-goots/o-tahg-gos-ehk
Ahnotes/ka-kee-se-khak

AUNT SHADIE stops the swing and takes VIOLET's hand. They turn and begin to walk into a shadowy forest.

SFX: Loud sound of pool balls being broken.

THE WOMEN suddenly turn their attention, song and focus on the bar. VERNA leads them into the bar.

VIOLET suddenly turns with the sound of the pool balls being broken and looks towards all the women walking in the bar.

VIOLET:
Can I go with them?

AUNT SHADIE:
No, you're too young. Besides, I need someone to walk with me.

VIOLET:
Heh? Who's that?

ROSE walks towards the two.

THE WOMEN:
See you as if you were sitting right here next to me
Ee-wa-pa-me-tan/tas-koots
Ota-e-iy-ya-pee-in

Below, the BARBER gets up, and VERNA follows him as he walks towards REBECCA, who rummages through her purse, takes out some money and leaves it on the table. She looks for something she thinks she's lost and dismisses it. She grabs her journal from the table just as VALERIE goes to look through it.

Under the water—under the earth
Eetam pehg/etam-as-keke

AUNT SHADIE:
I'll introduce you to *uppity*. That's Rose.

VIOLET:
  And I'm Violet.

AUNT SHADIE:
  Exactly. And I'm poopoo ka ka. Anyways ...

  ROSE reaches them and hugs VIOLET.

THE WOMEN:
  My body's floating where all the days are the same
  Ne-eow/e-pa-pam-mau-ho
  Tehk/eddie-tah-to-ke-sik
  Kow/pe-ya-kwun-nohk

  > *REBECCA walks towards the exit where RON is playing pool and MAVIS is making him look good.*

  Long and flowing like a river
  E-ke-knock/aqua/e-pe-mow-
  Ho-teak/tas-kooch/se-pe-h

VIOLET:
  She's squishing me.

AUNT SHADIE:
  She's hugging you.

VIOLET:
  No, she's squishing me.

AUNT SHADIE:
  Hugging—squishing. It's all the same thing.

VIOLET:
  The same what?

AUNT SHADIE:
  Love.

  MAVIS bumps RON and he stumbles into REBECCA, who drops her journal. Newspaper clippings of THE WOMEN fall to the floor. THE WOMEN slowly pick them up, look at themselves and then slowly place their clipping back into REBECCA's journal.

THE WOMEN:

My root—my heart
Weh-geese/ne dee

The BARBER reaches her table and looks down, as VERNA places REBECCA's wallet on the table. He looks around and puts it in his jacket. He watches as REBECCA begins to exit.

THE WOMEN shift all their energy towards the BARBER.

Lights begin to fade.

THE WOMEN:

My hair drifts behind me
Nes-ta-ga-yah/e-pim-mow
How-te-key

Lights out.

ACT 2

SLIDE: THE MORNING AFTER—Rebecca's Apartment— Kitsilano

It is dark in the bedroom. The neon face of the clock on the bedside table shows 4:08. It clicks.

A figure stirs in bed. A blue hue splashes down on white sheets and a figure underneath. REBECCA awakens.

REBECCA:

I remember drinking something blue, or was it thinking something blue? All I know right now is ... I have to pee. That means I have to get up, which means *you* have to ... get up. Get up, I dare you. Get up.

Her body doesn't move.

I'd like to lie here for an eternity, but I feel like I've eaten a squirrel and I need something to wash it down, and something to scrape it off my tongue. Don't feed the squirrels—eat them. Brilliant. Okay, I'm getting up, which means we're getting up.

THE WOMEN sit or stand in the darkness. They can be vaguely seen, but REBECCA cannot really see or really hear

*them. MAVIS now sits with her chair firmly attached to her
ass, as one.*

*REBECCA's body gets up, protesting. She stumbles through
her bedroom. She makes walking, stumbling curses. She stubs
her toe on the foot of the bed.*

REBECCA:
Ahhwww ... fuuuuuuuuuck, that hurts. Fuck you, bed.

MAVIS:
Watch where you're going, big feet.

REBECCA:
(*to herself*) Big Foot.

*She walks through her bedroom into the hallway, not
turning the lights on but doing the blind wall-feel.*

VERNA:
Right on my little toe. Not this way or that, but right on
my baby toe.

VALERIE:
This ... is a handicapped zone.

MAVIS:
Well, you better hope she doesn't park on your toe.

VALERIE:
Oh yeah. Too late—she just parked on my toe with the
corn. What the hell is this?

VERNA:
It's the fuckin' toe walk.

REBECCA walks into the wall, forehead first.

REBECCA:
Fuuuuck ouch ... Fuck you, wall.

ALL:

> Fuck you, big head.

REBECCA:

> (*to wall*) What did you say?

> *Nothing. Silence.*

> That's what I thought you said.

VALERIE:

> (*mimicking*) That's what I thought you said.

> *REBECCA reaches the fridge and opens the door. A bright light filters through like a tunnel, revealing the insides of the fridge and the inside of her apartment. THE WOMEN are all seated in a line. They are in various hues of shadow and dressed in white. Their hair is short.*

REBECCA:

> Ouch! Shit, that hurts.

VALERIE:

> Wow, let there be light.

· VERNA:

> And there was light ... I remember that.

> *REBECCA squints inside her fridge. Picks up a carton and tilts it back in a drink. Picks up another carton and another and another.*

VALERIE:

> Let there be skim milk.

VERNA:

> And there was none.

VALERIE:

> Let there be orange juice.

VERNA:

And there was none.

VALERIE:

Let there be water.

VERNA:

And there was none. Shit, she's making me have to go to the bathroom.

REBECCA closes the fridge door. Darkness. She stumbles along to the bathroom. She sits down on the can and takes a pee. The sound of a long pee.

MAVIS:

You think she could close the door.

VERNA:

You think she could go for me?

REBECCA:

Oh, that feels good.

REBECCA flushes the toilet.

MAVIS:

At least she didn't do number two.

VERNA:

At least she didn't do number two while reading a newspaper.

VALERIE:

Only men do that.

VERNA:

Women read novels.

MAVIS:

Like what?

VALERIE:

Well, real smart novels. They leave it in the can so they can make themselves look good.

MAVIS:

Like what?

VERNA:

I actually finished the whole AA Bible. Not one day at a time but one shit at a time. It took me a year ... if you were going to ask.

MAVIS:

I wasn't going to ask, but since you answered—why did it take you so long?

VERNA:

I kept having to introduce myself. There was always a big silence after I said, "Hi, my name's Verna." It left me kinda empty.

ALL:

Hi, Verna.

VERNA:

Thanks.

REBECCA gets herself to the front of the sink. The loud sound of her brushing her teeth. The sound of her taking a drink from the tap. She reaches over to turn the bathroom light on. When the bathroom lights blast on, the images of all three WOMEN reflect back in the mirror. REBECCA looks closely in the mirror.

THE WOMEN scream in horror.

REBECCA:

Wo-ow ... I look like shit.

REBECCA turns off the light.

ALL:

> Speak for yourself.

The sound of REBECCA returning on her journey back to bed in the darkness.

MAVIS:

> Ouch …

VERNA:

> Ouch …

VALERIE:

> Fuck! Oh yeah … right on the same toe, why don't yah!

REBECCA crawls into bed. Grabs her pillow and pulls it closer to herself. She pulls it closer and feels it. She feels it harder, her hand exploring it. It has legs. It has a butt. It has a penis.

IT moans. REBECCA screams.

IT:

> Hey …

REBECCA:

> Oh, fuck me!

VERNA:

> Too late.

VALERIE:

> The penis talks.

REBECCA jumps out of bed and turns on the bedroom light.

IT:

> Hey, what did you do that for?

They squint at each other.

REBECCA:

It's time to get up. I mean ... I mean ... it's time for you to get out. Leave.

MAVIS:

That's cold.

VERNA:

I like it. Thanks, and it's time to get up. Get in, get out ... and it's time to leave. It's to the point. Move on.

REBECCA:

Listen. I'm having a really bad morning.

IT:

Well, you had a really good night.

REBECCA:

If you say so.

IT:

You said so.

REBECCA:

That's really ... special ... but I have um ... I have to get myself together here pretty soon and go to work. Work is good. Work.

IT:

You don't work.

REBECCA:

Everybody works. You're right. I don't work. I write. Writing is work, and I really should work or write and um ... it's not easy to write when ...

IT:

You have a strange man in your bed.

REBECCA:

I was going to say, when there are people around.

IT:

Oh.

REBECCA:

Are you strange?

IT:

Okay ... I'm not strange. I'm a stranger.

REBECCA:

That's better. At least you're not weird.

IT:

Who's to know?

REBECCA:

Okay, if you weren't a stranger, would I know you were weird even if I knew you? I mean, does anybody ever know anybody's true weirdness?

IT:

This is weird.

REBECCA:

This is hurting my head, Ted.

IT:

It's Ron.

REBECCA:

I know ... it was just a rhyming thing. Yeah, Ron ... Ron (*to herself*) ... Ron with the nice butt leaning over the table.

MAVIS:

Turn over, Ron. Turn over a new leaf.

REBECCA:

You were playing ... we ended up playing pool.

RON:

You're surprised I'm here.

REBECCA:

Well, no. I mean, yes … I mean, who wouldn't be
surprised? A guy like you. A girl like me. Listen, I'm
swimming here. Let's just call this a day. Okay, Ron.
Thanks, it was great. Really. Ron. It was great. Great.

RON:

What was great?

REBECCA:

Oh, you know—the conversation, the beautiful dinner,
your great car … your great suit, how you put yourself
together, your great words, your greatness, your all-over
greatness … your money … your tireless dick. Is that
good? You are great. Great.

THE WOMEN:

Tireless dick? Let's see the great dick.

RON:

We didn't do it.

REBECCA:

O-kay … it just looks like we did.

RON:

Well, there was a point when that was an option, but …

REBECCA:

What?

RON:

You started crying.

REBECCA:

People do that sometimes.

RON:

When they're making love?

REBECCA:

No, when they're fucking and it reminds them of love.

RON/THE WOMEN:

Ouch.

REBECCA:

Sorry.

Silence.

Listen ... I don't mean to be rude ...

MAVIS:

... Maybe just a little peek ...

REBECCA:

... but I'm really not at my best right now, and maybe you should just leave.

RON:

What's your best?

REBECCA:

Coffee, fresh-squeezed orange juice, eggs benedict, morning sex ...

RON:

Do you bring a lot of men home?

REBECCA:

What, to mother? No, RON, I don't bring a lot of men home. Actually, you are the first man I've thought to bring HOME in ten years. And really, what if I did? What if I liked sleeping with men? What if I enjoyed sleeping with men so much I slept with men? What then, RON ... would that make me a slut? Or better yet, maybe I should've let you buy me a steak and potato and a bottle of plaid wine, and *you* could at least feel decent ...

He buries his head in the sheets.

Don't go to Sunday mass on me now, Ronny. (*he looks up*) I would get a good meal and a plaid wine, and you could feel like you *deserved* to fuck me. Fuck you, Ronny, and fuck the full meal deal.

RON:
  Are you finished?

REBECCA:
  I'm tired. I need a nap.

RON:
  Come here.

REBECCA:
  It's okay.

RON:
  Come here.

REBECCA:
  It's okay, I said.

RON:
  It's o-kay.

She goes towards him.

REBECCA:
  Okay. Don't you have a job?

RON:
  A day off.

REBECCA:
  Of?

RON:

    I'm a cop.

REBECCA:

    A cop.

RON:

    A problem?

THE WOMEN:

    A problem.

REBECCA:

    No, just weird. I don't usually do men with badges.

    They finally settle and fall asleep.

    REBECCA and RON settle into each other and fall asleep.
    THE WOMEN turn the lights off and walk into the living
    room. Lights up in the living room.

MAVIS:

    A cop.

VALERIE:

    You ever do a cop?

VERNA:

    Well, if I would have known they have nice butts and
    tireless dicks, I would've reconsidered.

MAVIS:

    A dick is a dick.

VALERIE:

    ... Is a dick.

VERNA:

    Is a prick.

MAVIS:

> I always kinda fantasized about it though ... kinda like a Harlequin Romance set in Canada. The Mountie, the horse and the Indian maiden.

VERNA:

> Exactly—the horse and the Indian maiden.

VALERIE:

> The Mountie probably just be watching.

VERNA:

> You'd probably have a better time with the horse anyways ...

MAVIS:

> You ever seen a horse's di ...

VALERIE:

> Too much of a good thing.

MAVIS:

> You said that kinda fast.

VERNA:

> Maybe a Mountie with a dick the size of a horse.

MAVIS:

> Dream on.

VALERIE:

> I am.

VERNA:

> Thanks ... now I'm getting all horny here. Let's make some tea and talk about our exes or something ... that should calm us down.

> *They follow each other into the kitchen. A kettle is set down and begins to heat. Lights out. Steam forms.*

SLIDE: *VIOLET DREAMS*

Lights slowly up on a figure above REBECCA's bed. The lights are different hues of violet. VIOLET is on a swing, slowly swinging back and forth above REBECCA's bed. She drops small pebbles over them as she talks.

VIOLET:

She's sleeping. Dreaming parts of worlds, yours and mine and hers. Dreaming and pressing into things ... old memories and loves and waking in moments wondering where people ended and why even in sleep it hurts. Even in sleep, it occurs and reoccurs and you wake half here, half there, everything separated.

REBECCA:

Everything not quite there, because you can't quite touch your own loss. Because it is so hollow.

VIOLET:

So ...

REBECCA:

... so far away—when you scream, it echoes.

VIOLET:

Oh, Jesus, we have all died for our sins.

REBECCA:

... Oh, Jesus, you say ...

VIOLET:

... we have all died for our sins.

REBECCA:

There are great days when everything is perfect. Cool days on your skin, when the breeze hits you just right and you can touch and taste the lips of those you loved. Cool, beautiful days when a tint of colour touches you ... just so. Just so.

VIOLET:

    … Just so lovely.

    VIOLET places a petal on REBECCA's lips.

REBECCA:

    You want to feel it on your lips forever. Just so. Just so until it ends, and all you can do is put your hand over your mouth. Gulping down the loss. Gulping down … down until you eat the scream. Blood vowels getting stuck between the sheets and pillows, between his legs and your throat, and all you want to do is say: Please help me. Please help me. Do you remember me? Because I remember me. I remember everything. Everything. Everything. And I can't breathe. And I would gladly die if I knew any better, but there is nothing to do but keep gulping silently. And it hurts my throat and God I want everything. I want to place my face in my mother's palm and say … and feel my lips on her lifeline and palm softness and whisper … I love you, you fucking bitch. I love you and where is everyone.

    SFX: THE WOMEN's kettle screams from the kitchen.

    The violet lights slowly fade and cross-fade, bringing purple on …

    SLIDE: SWITCHBOARD—Reception

    AUNT SHADIE and ROSE move around a large family table, setting it for tea. They stop to notice the switchboard and get caught up in its flashing beauty. The calls are lighting up different hues of purple.

ROSE:

    It's so beautiful.

AUNT SHADIE:

    It gives me a headache.

ROSE:

If you sit in a room and sit in a room ... pretty soon ...
(*she listens*) you can hear noises and voices coming
through the wallpaper like a whole bunch of flowers
sitting on a kitchen table. You become a part of that
family of sounds just by hearing them. You can hear
them eating and arguing, loving and fighting and
breathing.

AUNT SHADIE:

And snoring.

ROSE:

And ... snoring.

AUNT SHADIE:

Is that why you became a switchboard operator?

ROSE:

Partly.

AUNT SHADIE:

The other part?

ROSE:

It was a job, but after a while it made me a part of
something bigger than my own loneliness. As if every
time I connected someone I had found an answer.

AUNT SHADIE:

I've heard her voice through the wall. As if I've had my
ear to her as she's grown up. Just listening, not touching.
Not able to soothe her, even when she was a child,
because I wasn't there.

ROSE:

Maybe she was listening back to you.

AUNT SHADIE:

I didn't want her to see me the way he began to look at me. It wasn't that he said anything cruel, but men can be cruel with the twist of their face. I could feel myself disappearing, becoming invisible in his eyes; and when I looked in the mirror, what I held good like a stone deep inside was gone. I could no longer see myself. In life, you see yourself in how the people you love see you, and I began to hate seeing myself through his eyes. I began to hate my reflection. The stone though … loved his strong arms and body, loved the way his body tanned to meet mine in the summer times, loved the way he used to love me. I thought my silence complemented his voice, thought my redness, my stone, gave him weight. I have this child—light and dark, old and new. I place my stone in her and I leave. I was afraid she would begin to see me the way he saw me, the way white people look up and down without seeing you—like you are not worthy of seeing. Extinct, like a ghost … being invisible can kill you.

ROSE:

I see you, and I like what I see.

AUNT SHADIE:

I see you—and don't worry, you're not white.

ROSE:

I'm pretty sure I'm white. I'm English.

AUNT SHADIE:

White is a blindness—it has nothing to do with the colour of your skin.

ROSE:

You're gonna make me cry.

AUNT SHADIE:

You better make us some tea then.

ROSE:

That will help?

AUNT SHADIE:

No, but it gives you something to do.

*ROSE goes through her serious ritual of making tea. The
violet lights fade and cross-fade to REBECCA's bed. They light
up the bed like the bottom of a river, rocks scattered, rocks
curled. VALERIE and VERNA have come back to the bed
riverside. They are sitting around drinking tea, looking like
large boulders. They laugh and sing softly. VIOLET eventually
comes down from the swing, childlike.*

SLIDE: SHE SLEEPS LIKE A ROCK

REBECCA:

My heaviness has shifted—I'm all lopsided. Right now, I
am deep down lying between friends, tumbling over
each other, because we are round and hard and loving
every minute of it, because it is so far down the only
language we have to know has molded from the earth—
its tears and blood, its laughter and love—gone solid. I
hold it in my heart, it keeps me attached to the gravity of
a perfect knowing.

VALERIE:

A mother opens the heart of her child and places her
rock inside the flesh. Inside, so no one—no man, no
ugliness, will ever place its grabby hands on it.

VERNA:

A mother buries its knowledge inside the child. Kiss-
ageeta-ooma. It drops inside the eternity of blood and
earth. Kiss-ageeta-ooma. I love you, silly face.

REBECCA:

It makes me hit the riverbed like a rock. Water shining
over me new, over me new, a new reflection of my true
self, knowing I am heavy.

VALERIE:

A mother opens the heart of her child and places her rock inside the flesh. A growing child takes a rock from the earth it walked from and places it in a leather pouch and hangs it around her neck. A woman walks heavy.

VIOLET:

She sleeps like a rock.

VERNA:

She sleeps like a rock.

VIOLET:

She dreams like a rock.

VERNA:

She dreams like a rock.

VALERIE:

A woman walks heavy. A woman walks heavy. Like a rock molded from the earth—its tears and blood, its laughter and love—gone solid.

SLIDE: THE LIVING ROOM

MAVIS is at REBECCA's desk. She goes through her phone book and dials a number. AUNT SHADIE picks up the phone from the switchboard.

MAVIS:

Hi, Aunt Shadie.

AUNT SHADIE:

Verna?

MAVIS:

No, it's me … Mavis. We're a little late.

AUNT SHADIE:

Get your ass home.

MAVIS:

Don't yell at me—I'm the one who's considerate.

AUNT SHADIE:

I tell you, Rose is making tea for everyone …

MAVIS:

(*pinched operator's voice*) "To continue your call, please deposit more coins in the telephone or we'll have to …"

AUNT SHADIE:

Don't even try that with me.

VERNA walks in from the bedroom.

MAVIS:

Pardon me. You want to talk to Verna?

VERNA nodding her head—no, no, no.

Aunt Shadie wants to talk to you. Seriously.

VERNA:

Hi, Aunt Shadie.

AUNT SHADIE:

Like I was telling Mavis, get your asses home.

VERNA:

We just got caught up. Like I told you, we'll be up there in thir-tee minutes. Seriously. Thirty minutes.

She screams out for VALERIE.

Hey, Valerie, it's Pizza Hut. What kind of toppings do you want on your pizza. Here, you talk to them … I don't get what they're saying. They're talking too fast. Like you said, us Salish girls aren't so bright.

VALERIE marches in and grabs the phone. VIOLET follows.

VALERIE:

> We want everything. We want the special. Give us the special. Give us two specials. Hey, do you have any two-for-one specials?

> *VIOLET walks in from the bedroom.*

VIOLET:

> Ham and pineapple.

AUNT SHADIE:

> You're gonna get something real goddamned special when you all get home.

> *VALERIE puts the receiver against her chest.*

> *SFX: Muffled voice blabbing away.*

VALERIE:

> I don't think this is Pizza Hut.

VIOLET:

> Why?

VALERIE:

> Because Pizza Hut just swore. You can never make Pizza Hut swear.

VIOLET:

> How do you know?

VALERIE:

> Because, sometimes when I'm bored, I phone them up and play with them.

VIOLET:

> Like how?

VALERIE:

> Well, I ask what they got and then I ask 'em if they have any pizza made with bannock and then I pretend I

forget what they got and then I ask them what they got, what certain toppings are, and then anyways it goes on quite awhile. Indians aren't as much stupid as they are aggravating.

VERNA:

It's not Pizza Hut, stupid. It's Aunt Shadie.

VALERIE:

I thought I recognized her voice.

VERNA:

Here, you talk to her. She won't yell at you, because you're a baby.

VERNA picks up the receiver, listens to it and pushes it on VIOLET. VERNA goes into another room.

VIOLET:

Hi, Aunt Shadie. It's Violet. How are you? We're fine. We're all good. No, we're just hanging around. You know, talking and stuff. How's Rose?

AUNT SHADIE:

Save it.

VIOLET:

She said save it.

VALERIE:

She's pissed.

AUNT SHADIE:

Rose made tea for everyone, and now it's cold and ...

VIOLET:

(*to VALERIE*) Rose made tea for everyone and now ...

VALERIE:

Who cares? She's a weird duck anyways ... she can take the Red Rose manifest destiny and shove it up her ass ...

VIOLET:

... a teapot.

VALERIE:

Exactly. Free the leaves, baby. Free the tea leaves of Canada. Say goodbye already ... we'll be there as soon as we can.

VIOLET:

Goodbye already ... we'll be there as soon as we can. Aunt Shadie, sorry about the tea ...

AUNT SHADIE:

Just you hold it a ...

Click of phone.

VIOLET:

Sorry.

VALERIE:

Where's Verna? She's awfully quiet all of a sudden.

VIOLET:

She's always quiet.

VALERIE:

Just because a person doesn't say anything doesn't mean they're quiet. I can hear her thinking all the time. Where's Mavis? Now, her silence scares me. You know there's something wrong when you can't hear her talking.

They tiptoe around and peek in the bedroom. MAVIS is on the bed just about to pull the sheet off of RON's ass.

VALERIE:

Mavis, you pervert.

MAVIS:

I was just lookin', it's not like I was going to touch it or anything.

VALERIE:
Go ahead, I dare you.

MAVIS:
I dare you.

VALERIE:
Shit, I wouldn't touch anything that beige.

VIOLET:
Why?

VALERIE:
Jesus, Violet, you don't want to be lookin' at that.

VIOLET:
Why?

VALERIE:
You might go blind.

MAVIS:
I thought that's what happened when you masturbated.

VALERIE:
Well, you should know.

MAVIS:
Like ... I ... said. I thought that's what happened when you masturbated—I never heard of anyone going blind by touching a white ass.

VALERIE:
You shouldn't say masturbate in front of the kid.

MAVIS:
Masturbate, masturbate, masturbate. Why?

VIOLET looks at VALERIE intensely.

VALERIE:
It's a big word ... with a ... lot of responsibility.

MAVIS:
Number one, she's not a kid—she just seems like one.

VALERIE:
Well, maybe this isn't an ass—it just seems like one.

MAVIS:
Only one way to find out. Touch it.

VALERIE:
You touch it.

MAVIS:
No, you touch it.

VALERIE:
Scared of the real thing? You've been dying for it for so long. Go crazy.

MAVIS:
You go crazy.

VALERIE pinches it hard.

RON:
Oh!

RON wakes up and looks around. The clock neons 6:30. He crawls out of bed. Walks around the living room and picks up a newspaper and walks to the bathroom and shuts the door.

MAVIS:
Now he's gonna take a shit and stink up the place.

VALERIE:
Let a guy into your bedroom, and he thinks he can take a big dump in your can.

MAVIS:

I bet he turns on the fan.

Sound of the toilet flushing and bathroom fan turns on.

VALERIE:

Like that's gonna help.

They wait. Silence. Smell. They both start waving their hands in front of their face like a fan.

Shiiiiiiiiiiit …

VIOLET starts looking for VERNA. VERNA wants to be alone and is sitting slumped down against a wall. VIOLET sits down next to her.

VIOLET:

Why do you think we're here?

VERNA:

Is this the BIG question? Because, if it is … I'm not up to it, okay? Why don't you go ask "Know It All" Mavis or something?

VIOLET:

I'm asking you.

VERNA:

And I'm telling you I don't know. I mean, why is anybody anybody? Why does anybody end up anywhere? Why does … I never figured it out, okay. I just don't know … if I knew I wouldn't be here or maybe I would. I just don't know.

VIOLET:

Why don't you know?

VERNA:

Why don't you shut up?

VIOLET:
You don't have to be mean.

VERNA:
(*in a whiny voice*) Why is the world mean? Why doesn't
Mommy love me? Why is Daddy touching me there?
Why? Why? I don't know. Why me?

VIOLET:
Why aren't you nice?

VERNA:
(*raises her voice*) Why aren't you in bed?

VIOLET:
Why are you yelling?

VERNA:
I'm not yelling.

VIOLET:
Why are you mad?

VERNA:
Because I'm dead, and I'm still thirsty.

VIOLET:
Thirsty?

> *VERNA leans over and screams at her silently.*

VERNA:
THIRSTY, you fuckin' parrot. I'm thirsty for ... for ... my
kids, my man. I'm thirsty, thirsty, thirsty, THIR-sty,
THIRSTY, dehydrated, dry, parched, thirsty. Get IT?

VIOLET:
You didn't have to get mad. (*VIOLET puts her head down
and pouts*)

VERNA:

(*lowers her voice and gets up*) It's the only way I know how to get from here ... to there.

VIOLET looks up, and VERNA has disappeared. VERNA makes her way to the Empress Hotel.

RON walks through all the WOMEN with coffee. They all stop and look at his parts.

SLIDE: THE MORNING AFTER—Continued.

RON walks into the bedroom with two cups of coffee. He hands one to REBECCA.

RON:

I made some coffee. You don't have any cream. You have a carton, but you don't have any cream.

REBECCA:

That doesn't surprise me.

RON:

So.

REBECCA:

So. Ron. How are you this morning?

RON:

I feel like shit.

REBECCA:

Well, since we're doing the true confession part of the morning—me too.

RON:

You were talking in your sleep ... and you pinched my ass.

REBECCA:

I talk in my sleep, but it wasn't me who pinched your ass.

RON:

> I pinched my own ass.

REBECCA:

> Stranger things have happened. Maybe you were feeling hard done by.

RON:

> I am actually, but that's another story. What were you doing down there?

REBECCA:

> The Empress? Thinking and drinking. What were you doing down there?

RON:

> Drinking and playing pool. We usually go in after work and have a couple of beers. Why do you drink there?

REBECCA:

> Well, I don't always drink there, but it's a good place to go and think, and I can usually have a drink in quiet without some suit coming up and trying to dazzle me. The worst thing that can happen is an old beat-up suit will sit down and try and dazzle me, which is usually more sad than it is offensive. Besides, I am looking for someone.

RON:

> Who—Mr. Right?

REBECCA:

> I married Mr. Right. And divorced Mr. Right. So, now I'm looking for Mr. Fun.

RON:

> So, who are you looking for really?

REBECCA:

I'm looking for my mom. She went for a walk twenty years ago, and I haven't seen her since.

RON:

And you think she's down there.

REBECCA:

Yup.

RON:

Why?

REBECCA:

She was last seen down there.

RON:

Why now?

REBECCA:

Why now what?

RON:

Why do you want to find her now?

REBECCA:

I'm not mad anymore.

RON:

Remind me not to make you mad.

REBECCA:

Well, sometimes it helps to be mad.

RON:

You think she's down there. Like living down there? It's not the greatest place to live.

REBECCA:

No, really?

RON:

I'm just saying the people who live down there are mostly drunks and junkies and Ind ... First Na ...

REBECCA:

And what? You were going to say Indians. Oh, don't get all politically correct on me now ...

RON:

Okay, Indians. You got a thing for Indians?

REBECCA:

Yeah, I got a thing for Indians. You got a thing against Indians?

RON:

No, I was just saying ...

REBECCA:

Never mind. Save it for your job.

RON:

What's that supposed to mean?

REBECCA:

Listen. I'm not really into Education 101 this morning. So why don't you take your pale bum home.

RON:

Let me guess ... you're Indian.

REBECCA:

Part Indian.

RON:

Which part?

REBECCA:

The good part.

RON:

I thought you were Italian or something.

REBECCA:

I thought you were white or something. And I was right.
So we both win.

RON:

It's just that you don't seem Indian.

REBECCA:

That begs the question—what does an Indian seem like?
Let me guess—you probably think that, if an Indian
goes to university or watches T.V., it makes them the
same as every other Canadian. Only less. The big
melting pot. The only problem is you can't melt an
Indian. You can't kill a stone. You can grind it down to
sand, but it's still there sifting through everything
forever. There, you got it.

RON:

Wow, and it's not even nine o'clock in the morning.

REBECCA:

I haven't even finished my first cup of coffee.

RON:

Since you're there, why do you think so many end up
down there?

REBECCA:

Since you asked, I don't think so many of them end up
down there. I think so many people end up down there.
Period.

RON:
Why?

REBECCA:

It's an accident. Something heavy falls on them. It might just be one Thing ... one thing and then everything seems to tumble down and pretty soon there is no getting up.

RON:

What do you mean?

REBECCA:

Like an accident—people drive by in their nice cars and stare at people on those streets, because they realize for a moment it could happen to them. So they might be saying "poor bastards," but what they're really thinking about is themselves and their own potential tragedy.

So these nice people finally look away and—to console themselves from that one conscious thought—think it couldn't happen to them. It's happening to "those" people. Even better if "those" people are mentally ill or brown or addicted to one thing or another. Because these nice people can park their nice cars in their nice driveways and open the doors to their nice homes and take a couple of nice Valiums, or call up that nice Betty Ford and go for a nice little vacation "just to get away." They think they are safe. It doesn't matter where your room is—you still have to face the face.

RON:

The room?

REBECCA:

Yourself. Alone.

RON:

So you're saying that's why people end up there.

REBECCA:

Yes, they're alone and they know it but there's nothing more comforting than being with a group of people who know they are alone ...

RON:

... It's like going to hear the blues when you're feeling like shit. It makes you feel better.

REBECCA:

(*she looks at him*) Yeah ...

RON:

Gotcha.

REBECCA:

Well, this has been a lot of fun, but I really have to get a move on.

RON:

That means I have to leave.

REBECCA:

That means—yeah ... you have to leave. I have to get dressed. Day stuff.

RON:

Can I give you a call?

REBECCA:

Mmmmm?

RON:

Maybe I could take you out for supper.

REBECCA:

Steak and potato and a good red wine.

RON:

Sure ... make me an honest asshole.

REBECCA:

Make me an honest woman. My life is kinda clustered right now but ...

RON:

But ...

REBECCA:

Yeah ... maybe ... I think I've told you too much.

RON:

I don't think you've told me enough.

REBECCA:

Well, I wouldn't have told you anything, but I didn't think I'd see you again.

RON:

And now?

REBECCA:

I've probably said too much.

> RON *starts to get his clothes together and puts them on. He leaves. REBECCA rolls over to sleep.*

> **SLIDE: THE LIVING ROOM—Continued.**

> THE WOMEN *are in different areas of the apartment touching and using REBECCA's things. VALERIE is going through REBECCA's laundry that's lying in a basket. She's pulling out different pieces of underwear and trying them on. MAVIS is sitting at REBECCA's desk playing with the phone. VIOLET has been in REBECCA's bedroom swinging on her swing and playing with REBECCA's pretty things. Gradually, THE WOMEN pick what they want of REBECCA's clothing and make-up and put them on.*

MAVIS:

She's gonna know you were in her drawers. Women always know when someone's been in their drawers.

VALERIE:

So. Like, what's she gonna do about it?

MAVIS:

The point is—you shouldn't be wearing her underwear.
It doesn't even fit you.

VALERIE:

It fits parts of me. And why don't you get off your ass
and find out where Verna went?

MAVIS:

I will after ... I finish this one last call.

VALERIE:

Who the hell are you talking to anyways?

MAVIS:

Talked to my Aunt Bertha. She died when I was eight.
She thought I'd forgotten all about her, but I said I
always remembered her on account she told me I was
beautiful when I was little. I always remember people
who said I was beautiful.

VALERIE:

Well, that's got to be real hard on your memory.

MAVIS:

What?

VALERIE:

I said, are you going to see where Verna is or do I have
to?

MAVIS:

You have to.

VALERIE doesn't leave but eavesdrops on MAVIS's conversation.

MAVIS:

Hi … Dad. It's me. Mavis. Well, I just thought I'd call and say hi. No reason. Like I said, I just got to thinking about you and thought—what the hell, I'll just give the old man a call just out of the blue. How have you been? (*she shrugs*) How do I think you've been? Well, good I guess. Dad? Geez, he hung up on me.

VALERIE:

What did you expect?

MAVIS:

I thought he would've mellowed a bit in death.

VALERIE sniffs the air, and VIOLET tiptoes back into the room.

VALERIE:

I think she's been into the perfume.

MAVIS:

How do you know?

VALERIE:

Can't you smell her coming?

MAVIS:

Geez, she smells like an old whore.

VALERIE:

What's that supposed to mean?

MAVIS:

Just that she stinks I guess.

VIOLET:

She's got lots of perfume.

VALERIE:

We know.

VIOLET:

I love perfume. I always wanted lots of perfume. That a drop could make you smell good all over, feel good all over, is kinda amazing.

VALERIE:

That's the way I feel about lingerie. I got my first real bra when I was 12, you know one of those God-ugly white things from the Sears catalogue. The first day I came to the city, I went into a lingerie store—it was the most beautiful thing. Red and silk and satin and nylons and things that went up your butt and things that went down your butt and pulled things together and separated other things. That's a fuckin' miracle happening if you ask me. I guess lingerie was my downfall.

MAVIS:

How so?

VALERIE:

I always wanted to show it to people.

MAVIS:

Give me a pair of clean cotton undies any day.

VALERIE:

What do you know about lingerie? You never get *off* your ass to appreciate anything *on* your ass.

MAVIS:

Listen, Valerie ... enough about my ass, okay?

VALERIE:

Okay, okay—touchy, touchy.

MAVIS:

... And since you're worried about everybody's ass, go and see if Verna's in the can.

VALERIE moves towards the bathroom.

VALERIE:

> Probably reading her one-shit-at-a-time AA book. A
> capital-letter SOB story if you ask me.

VIOLET:

> She's not in there.

MAVIS:

> So now what?

VALERIE:

> Well, I guess we look good enough to go look for her.

> *They stop and look in REBECCA's mirror. They put on the
> finishing touches of make-up and scarves, etc. They look
> good. They turn to go.*

> Ready?

MAVIS:

> Ready.

> *They leave. VIOLET picks up some red lipstick and puts it on.*

> *The phone rings. Lights up on REBECCA, as she mutters
> and gets up and picks up the phone. Lights up on AUNT
> SHADIE at the switchboard.*

REBECCA:

> Hello?

> *AUNT SHADIE—recognizing REBECCA's voice—stops, breathes
> slowly and sits down, not able to answer, cradling the phone.*

> Answer, why don't you?

> *Nothing.*

> (*sarcastically*) I love you too.

REBECCA places the receiver down. Lights out on AUNT SHADIE. REBECCA enters the bathroom and starts the shower and gets in.

The phone rings. She wraps herself and stumbles towards it dripping. She picks it up.

SFX: A male voice talking under.

REBECCA:

Ahhhh ... enough already. (*picks up phone*) Hello? Am I missing something? (*to herself*) Well, why don't we just play a little game. I'm not sure yet—why? Why didn't you just say that? I must've lost it when I was down there last night. Yeah, I'll be down this afternoon. How will I know you? Okay, yeah. I'll ask the bartender. You can tell me by the picture on my driver's license, or at least I hope you can. Thanks ... yeah this afternoon. I'll be there—I told you. Thanks.

She hangs up the phone.

(*to herself*) Weirdo.

REBECCA searches through her laundry basket for her new underwear. She looks under things, the search continues.

Oh, that's great. I finally get a set of great underwear, and the dryer eats it ... Here, underwear. Oh, this is not a good day. I should just go back to bed. Go back to bed. Okay, I can do it. Seventy dollars worth of gonch disappeared ... feeling like shit.

The phone rings. It's RON.

Hello. I mean ... (*sexy*) hel-lo. Just kidding. How you doing? I haven't seen you for at least a couple of hours. Dinner? What do you feel like eating? Steak. Perfect. No, great choice. How can I refuse when you say it like that? I have some running around to do today, but later tonight sounds good. Okay—see you then ... there ... whatever. Bye.

She gets up, walks past a mirror and looks in.

Feeling good ... looking like shit ... lost my wallet ... talking to myself ... and a slut to top it off. Perfect.

She walks into her bedroom. Stops suspiciously and looks at the bed's toes.

Don't even think about it if you want to live.

Lights down.

VIOLET makes her way slowly up the stairs.

SLIDE: SETTING THE TABLE

ROSE is going around the table placing plates.

ROSE:
You smell pretty. Do you want to help?

VIOLET:
Okay.

VIOLET picks up a pile of cutlery and begins handing it to her. AUNT SHADIE sits quietly by herself weaving snowshoes. She places her feet in each, testing them out. ROSE and VIOLET place the silverware in a setting ritual.

Why do you think we're here?

ROSE:
That's a big question.

VIOLET:
That's a big question—that's what everybody says.

ROSE:
I spent most of life waiting for the big answer. Waiting to fall in love, waiting to have children, waiting to give.

VIOLET:

Waiting for the right things to happen that would make everything alright.

ROSE:

Waiting.

VIOLET:

(*more like a woman than a child*) But not making a choice.

ROSE:

Sometimes the right moment in time ...

VIOLET:

The right waiting is our own making ...

ROSE:

... our knowing that everything has a time and a place.

AUNT SHADIE puts both snowshoes on and is practicing. Proud of her limbs and her snowshoe expertise.

AUNT SHADIE:

That we've never forgotten.

VIOLET holds the last knife for a moment and then places it on the table in its setting. She turns to look at AUNT SHADIE. AUNT SHADIE nods and VIOLET walks back down like a woman.

SLIDE: THE EMPRESSES

The BARBER sits at a red terry-cloth table sipping beer. He is dressed in a suit, though shabby around the edges. VERNA is seated beside him, leaning into him, talking. The BARBER is scoping out the place and oblivious to her chatter.

VERNA:

Listen, you moron. I'm talking to you. O Bald One. Don't think I even went around with you because you are good-looking or nothing—you're ugly. Ugly ... look at those glasses—four eyes—big eyes bulging out like you're looking at headlights or something. Big dumb ... Stupid.

VERNA slaps him upside the head. His glasses fall off. He picks them up and places them back on his head. The slap changes his focus. He looks through the bar where his barbershop slowly lights up. In a hunting hallucination, his instinct sharpens as he sees a flash of brown moving. He attempts to stumble up. VERNA sits him down roughly.

Not so fast, ree-tard. I got a few more things to get off my chest.

He staggers back down, his eyes fixated on an image coming through the mirrors of his barbershop. A forest forms in the mirrors. The flashes of brown become closer, getting clearer.

GILBERT:
Okay, baby ... that's it, baby ... that's it.

VERNA:
Nee.chin whikth quan.knit to squaw.kwaw—I already took the liquor.

He concentrates single-mindedly on his vision.

GILBERT:
Oh, it is brown—the colour of my thirst.

VERNA:
It's my drink—tay squaw.kaw.

The brown blurs form into a beautiful projection of MARILYN, PENNY and PATSY, who are dressed in their hair dreams, seductive and sensual. The projections accent their legs and limbs and eyes. VALERIE and MAVIS step into the image and slowly emerge from the mirror, beautifully in deer-like grace, in unison—part woman, part animal seduction. As they emerge, VIOLET follows behind them—high woman vogue. The following is a collage of images, song, language and movement. Intoxicating and potent.

Quaw.swhat.tus.at.na.ay. quee.quaw—as it reaches my stomach, Yoh hat.toe.know. a.tone.nas.new.whakt—of my sacred beliefs.

VALERIE and MAVIS get closer to him, moving slowly and sensually. They stop to apply lipstick seductively, suggestively, for him.

Thirsty for living.

GILBERT:
I watched.

They stop mid-lipstick.

VERNA:
Thirsty.

THE WOMEN:
I held my breath.

GILBERT:
Like animals before her, she was there when I needed to take.

VERNA:
Hungry.

THE WOMEN seductively pour beer down his throat.

THE WOMEN:
He was afraid of making a mistake.

VERNA:
Hungry.

GILBERT:
Like animals before her, I wished to look in her eyes …

He tries to pull VALERIE closer. VALERIE places her lips on his and feeds him beer.

VERNA:
Hungry.

THE WOMEN:
I saw the smallness.

VERNA:
... Lies ...

GILBERT:
I took them before they could really see me.

VERNA:
In desperation.

They sniff.

THE WOMEN:
I smelt him.

VERNA:
Hungry for me.

GILBERT:
Like animals before her, there was a stillness.

He staggers for them. They pull away. Stop.

VERNA:
My heart.

They stop and sigh.

THE WOMEN:
... A stillness ...

VERNA:
The real me.

THE WOMEN:
   ... a peacefulness ...

VERNA:
   Waiting.

GILBERT:
   A gasp.

   They pose and sigh.

VERNA:
   Waiting.

GILBERT:
   Expecting ...

   They moan seductively.

VERNA:
   ... to laugh at ...

GILBERT:
   ... deliverance.

VERNA:
   ... Salvation.

   They walk away slowly, beautifully, eyes on him.

THE WOMEN:
   There was only my God laughing when he said ...

GILBERT:
   "... There are more ways than one to skin an animal."

THE WOMEN:
   There was only my God laughing when he said ...

GILBERT:
   "... Everyone thinks it, they just don't do it."

THE WOMEN:
There was only me laughing when he said …

GILBERT:
Die. Die.

THE WOMEN:
Only me.

VERNA:
Seeing …

GILBERT:
… the look in their eyes.

VERNA:
Pointing …

THE WOMEN:
… back …

VERNA:
Leaving you …

GILBERT:
… wondering—can an animal laugh?

VALERIE, MAVIS and VIOLET slip back into the mirror and through the images of MARILYN, PATSY and PENNY. The mirror reflecting many women.

THE WOMEN:
Oh yes. Oh yes. Forever.

GILBERT starts pounding his drinks, shaken.

GILBERT:
I am a good and decent man.
I am a good and good-living man.

MAVIS, VALERIE and VIOLET appear behind VERNA. VALERIE places her hand on VERNA's shoulder.

VALERIE:

    It's time to go, Verna—he's not worth it.

GILBERT:

    I am clean.

MAVIS:

    He's just a man.

GILBERT:

    I am.

VERNA:

    An ugly man to boot.

GILBERT:

    I am.

VIOLET:

    An ugly man to boot.

GILBERT:

    I am.

MAVIS:

    You should feel sorry for him.

GILBERT:

    Therefore, I am.

VERNA:

    Sorry? (*pause*) All I feel sorry for is his little dick and his ugly face. Besides, I'm tired of feeling sorry for white people.

    GILBERT continues to get blasted.

MAVIS:

    Okay, enough of this ugly.

VERNA:

What? You got something for him, Mavis?

MAVIS:

I never had anything for him, Verna. I thought he was someone else.

VERNA:

Well, that's easy to say now …

VALERIE:

That's enough, Verna. We all thought he was someone we knew. Someone we needed. Okay, leave it alone.

VERNA:

Skinny bastard.

MAVIS:

We should go, Verna.

VERNA:

You go.

VALERIE:

We're not leaving you here, Verna.

VERNA:

Why the hell not?

VALERIE:

It would be too pitiful.

VERNA:

You wanna make something out of this, Valerie?

VALERIE:

Verna, you know I could make you in a minute.

VERNA gets up from her chair to challenge VALERIE.

VERNA:

Make this …

MAVIS:

Hello—it's her Rebecca.

VALERIE / VIOLET:

Oh shittttttttttttttttttttt …

    REBECCA approaches them. THE WOMEN back away slightly.

REBECCA:

Excuse me?

THE WOMEN:

Ahhhh … yeah?

GILBERT:

(*hazy drunk*) Yeah? What do you want? (*he looks at her intensely*) I mean … how can I help you? Miss.

REBECCA:

Umm … the guy at the front said you were the one that had my wallet. I mean you were the one that found it. Remember, you told me to get the bartender to point you out.

GILBERT:

Right … right. Mind isn't what it used to be. (*laughs*) Have a seat.

    REBECCA sits.

I saw you in here last night. It must've fallen from your jacket or something. I'm just glad I could help.

VALERIE:

Help this, you fuckin' pig! (*she squeezes her boobs together*)

REBECCA:

Well, thanks. It's always a big hassle when you lose your I.D.

THE WOMEN:

I'll say.

GILBERT:

What's a nice girl like you hanging around a place like this?

MAVIS:

Oh, that's original.

REBECCA:

Just playing pool.

GILBERT:

Can I buy you a drink?

VIOLET:

No.

REBECCA:

No, it's okay.

GILBERT:

Seriously, you look like a lady that was lookin' for something.

He hands her over a beer. She watches the beer slide over.

REBECCA:

O-kay ... Well, it's a long story.

GILBERT:

I got all the time in the world.

REBECCA:

Really. I have been looking for my mother. She was last seen in this neighbourhood. Seems I just get close to where she last lived, or where she used to hang out, and I somehow miss her.

GILBERT:

You gotta picture? I've been around here for a long time.

REBECCA shuffles in her purse and pulls a picture out. She shows it to him. All the WOMEN look at it.

VALERIE:

Holy shit, she was beautiful.

MAVIS:

Kinda looks like me when I was young.

VERNA:

Yeah, right.

GILBERT:

I think I know her. I think her name was—well ... I don't know her real name, but they used to call her Aunt Shadie or something ...

REBECCA:

Aunt Shadie?

THE WOMEN:

Aunt Shadie?!

GILBERT:

Aunt Shadie. Come to think of it, I had a drink with her a while back.

REBECCA:

How long ago is a while back?

GILBERT:

I lose track of time—you know how it is? Anyways, she left some things with me to hold for safekeeping ... she said she was gonna try and look up a daughter she hadn't seen in a while. I'm always tryin' to help some of these women out.

REBECCA:

Really.

GILBERT:

If you want, we can finish these off and head over to my barbershop. I think I got something of hers there.

The BARBER watches her as REBECCA downs her beer. They get up, and he stumbles and tries to pull himself together. REBECCA looks around, she stops.

THE WOMEN:

It's alright.

REBECCA:

(*to herself, them*) It's alright.

Lights down.

SLIDE: WHEN SHE WAS HORNY AND WANTED SEX—*The Barbershop*

They enter the barbershop. GILBERT walks around and shuts the blinds to his storefront. REBECCA walks around the shop, keeping her distance. He stares intensely at her.

REBECCA:

It's a nice shop. Do you have a lot of clients?

GILBERT:

Just my regulars. They like the service I've always given them.

REBECCA:

I'm sure they do.

GILBERT:

I'm good at my job. Been doing it for thirty years now.

REBECCA:

Really?

GILBERT:

You could say this has been my calling.

REBECCA:

What do you like best about it?

GILBERT:

I'm in control, and I know what they want.

REBECCA:

What do they want?

GILBERT:

That depends.

REBECCA:

I love barbershops. Always loved them. Ever since I was a little girl I used to come with my dad and watch him get shaved and have his hair cut.

She touches his utensils.

GILBERT:

You used to have long hair?

REBECCA:

Yeah, but I cut it because I … you wouldn't understand. I cut it to my shoulders a couple of months ago. It will grow, and I'll braid it like I used to when I was a kid.

GILBERT:

Braids?

REBECCA:

My dad used to do it for me … he used to say I looked just like my mom when he finished. I used to love that.

GILBERT:
Can I braid it? I like women in braids.

REBECCA:
No, it's alright. Thanks ...

He grabs her hair from behind.

She grabs her hair back.

Enough.

GILBERT:
(*he turns. To himself*) You fuckin' uppity bitch.

REBECCA:
Pardon me?

GILBERT:
(*mimicking her*) Pardon me?

He gets out a bottle from his cupboard.

Do you want a drink?

REBECCA:
Sure, I guess. Shouldn't you be working?

GILBERT:
I am.

Long awkward silence.

REBECCA:
So ... can I see what you have of my mother's? I don't usually drink in the afternoon, so this is really a special treat. It really goes straight to my head ...

GILBERT:
Here, I'll just top you up.

REBECCA:

Yeah …

She watches him pour the drink.

GILBERT:

I'm just gonna go freshen up a bit. Don't want to be in
the company of a beautiful young woman looking like I
need to brush my teeth.

GILBERT exits to go to the bathroom.

REBECCA:

And you're only worried about your teeth … fuckin'
scary.

*She goes to pull out a drawer and then stops and looks at the
red-and-white barber light. She stops for a long moment and
breathes. She walks directly towards it, taking the bottom off
the light. A handful of long black braids fall to the floor. She
gasps and touches each one until she gets to her mother's. She
picks her mother's braid up and buries her face in it and
sobs. REBECCA hears GILBERT approaching. Shaken, she
takes her jacket off and covers the braids and tries to get
herself together.*

Here, Gilbert, why don't you have a seat. I always found
shaving men sexy. It makes me horny. Can I shave you,
Gilbert?

GILBERT:

I don't know … it's not usually how things work.

REBECCA:

Things they are a-changin' …

GILBERT:

What?

REBECCA:

Just a song I had in my head. Oh, come on.

GILBERT:

Okay … you have to be careful.

REBECCA:

I'll be gentle.

He reaches up to touch her. She grabs his hands.

You have beautiful hands. I've always loved men's hands. How they move. Your hands are so soft and white. I bet you've loved a lot of women.

GILBERT:

I've had my share of women.

REBECCA:

You're being modest.

GILBERT:

Women have always taken to me. I know how to make a woman happy. I know what they want to hear.

He places his hands on her breasts.

REBECCA:

Slow down, Gilbert. Slow down, we have lots of time. Would you like a drink? Can I buy you a drink? Can I get you a drink?

GILBERT:

What do you mean?

REBECCA:

I mean, can I pour you a drink?

GILBERT:

Sure, I guess.

REBECCA:

Here you go. You sure you don't want more? You look like you can handle your liquor.

GILBERT:

I'm not scared of anything.

She pours him a heap.

REBECCA:

Of course not. Okay, baby. Can I shave you?

GILBERT:

You have to be very careful.

REBECCA:

I'd never do anything to hurt you. Do you want your bottle? Here, why don't I place it right here, so it can be close to you? Do you like that? It's right here so it can be close to you. Do you like that?

She grooves it into his crotch. He moans.

I'll just place this over you now. Like this?

She places his barbershop cape over him. It covers his body.

GILBERT:

That's right.

REBECCA:

That's right.

He grabs her hand. She keeps him from forcing her hand down.

GILBERT:

That's right. Right down here ... you fuckin' ...

REBECCA:

Gilbert. Shhhhhhhh ... just wait ... just wait. Close your eyes and relax. Relax. I'm here, baby.

GILBERT:

Yeah. I'll relax when I'm stuffing you with my ...

REBECCA:

Should I use this? (*she grabs the shaving cream bottle*) So, I take it in my hand ... spray it out like this? You tell me, you're the professional.

GILBERT:

That's it. That's it. Jesus Christ, just do it.

REBECCA:

Just close your eyes—let me do all the work.

She smoothes the foam over his face sensually.

GILBERT:

Mmmmmm.

He closes his eyes. As she spreads the foam on his face, a forest reflects in the mirrors as it is being covered by billowing snow. A beautiful, crystallized snow scene.

A voice from the dark approaches through the landscape. It gets closer and closer. At first, just a movement and glimpses of brown.

AUNT SHADIE:

I used to be a real good trapper when I was young. You wouldn't believe it, now that I'm such a city girl. But before, when my legs and body were young and muscular, I could go forever. Walking those traplines with snowshoes. The sun coming down, sprinkling everything with crystals, some floating down and dusting that white comforter with magic. I would walk that trapline ...

REBECCA:

I would walk that trapline ...

AUNT SHADIE:

... like a map, my body knowing every turn, every tree, every curve the land uses to confuse us.

REBECCA:
> … like a map, my body knowing every turn, every lie, every curve they use to kill us.

REBECCA / AUNT SHADIE:
> I felt like I was part of the magic that wasn't confused.

REBECCA:
> The crystals sticking to the cold and the cold sticking to my black hair, my eyebrows, my clothes, my breath. A trap set.

> > *REBECCA braces herself. She takes the razor and is about to cut his throat.*

> An animal caught.

> > *The BARBER's eyes suddenly blaze open. He grabs her hand and they struggle with the blade. The blade draws closer to her neck and is about to cut her open.*

> > *AUNT SHADIE emerges from the landscape as a trapper. She stands behind REBECCA. She puts her hand over REBECCA's hand and draws the knife closer to the BARBER's neck. He looks up and panics as he sees AUNT SHADIE and THE WOMEN/TRAPPERS behind her. Squirming, they slit his throat.*

AUNT SHADIE:
> Red.

> > *They look at each other. Blood seeps on his white gown.*

REBECCA:
> Red.

AUNT SHADIE:
> If it squirmed, I would put it out of its misery as fast as I could.

THE TRAPPERS follow through, as REBECCA and her mother stare at each other. THE TRAPPERS take the razor, wash it and replace it. REBECCA hands each woman their braids. THE WOMEN leave in a line. Her mother remains standing. REBECCA reaches in her pocket and hands her mother her braid of hair.

AUNT SHADIE:
Re-becca.

AUNT SHADIE raises her hand and touches her face.

REBECCA:
Meegweetch and thank you.

AUNT SHADIE hugs her and falls behind the line of WOMEN/TRAPPERS. She falls in behind the rest of THE TRAPPERS, as the lights fade on the landscape and THE WOMEN tracking their way back.

SLIDE: THE FIRST SUPPER—NOT TO BE CONFUSED WITH THE LAST SUPPER

REBECCA watches the long line of women as they take their heavy trapping clothes off, their long, long hair spilling everywhere. They begin to sit down to a beautiful banquet à la the Last Supper. Lights fade on them, and the sound of their voices becomes the sound of trees.

SFX: Sound of tree leaves moving in the wind.

REBECCA exits from the barbershop. She walks in the wind and trees.

SFX: The loud sound of a tree falling ...

She stops and listens to the sound.

The barbershop is empty except for the BARBER in his chair. Barber lights swirl red and white throughout the barbershop. The red light intensifies and takes over the room.

Fade out.

SFX: The sound of the tree hitting the ground with a loud thud.

REBECCA closes her eyes for a moment and then continues walking.

Fade out.

THE END.